Wakefield Press

Days of Masks and Riddles

Franz Kempf as an artist, craftsman and teacher has a deep involvement with the arts and community. He has been associated with Jacob Pins in Israel, Oscar Kaskoschka in Europe and workshops all over Europe and Australia. A Fellow of the Royal Society (London) and the Graphic Society (U.S.A.), in 2003 he was awarded the Order of Australia for his services to the arts.

Days of
Masks and Riddles

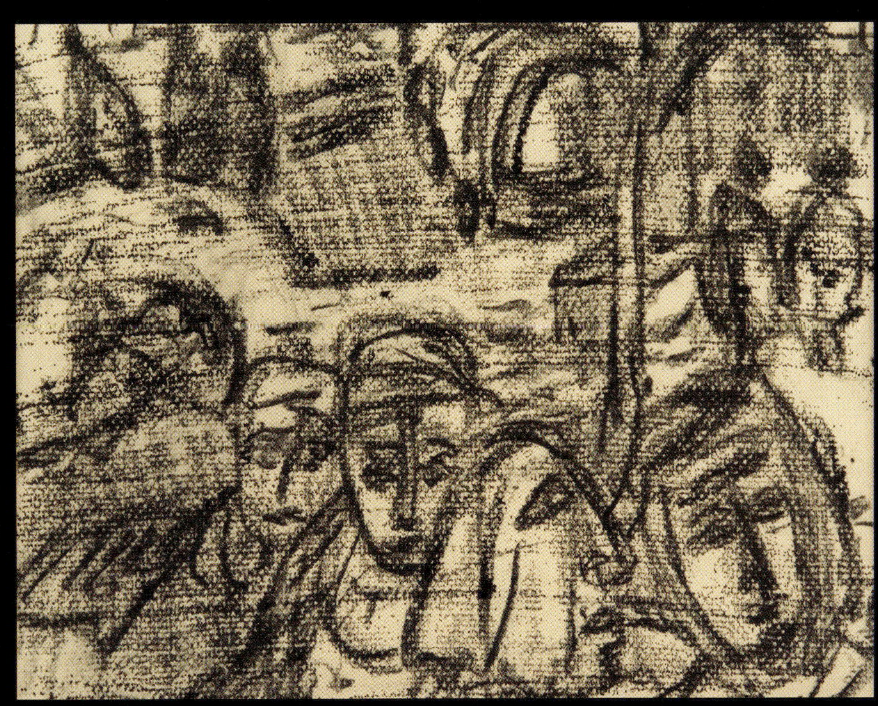

FRANZ KEMPF

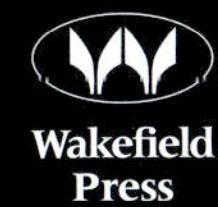

Wakefield
Press

Wakefield Press
1 The Parade West
Kent Town
South Australia 5067
www.wakefieldpress.com.au

First published 2010

Copyright © Franz Kempf, 2010

All rights reserved. This book is copyright. Apart from any fair dealing for the purposes of private study, research, criticism or review, as permitted under the Copyright Act, no part may be reproduced without written permission. Enquiries should be addressed to the publisher.

Designed by Dean Lahn, Lahn Stafford Design
Printed in Australia by Ligare Pty Ltd

ISBN 978 1 86254 941 8

Days of Masks and Riddles reflects aspects of a journey through a world of the imagination – of light and darkness, of war, chaos and natural disasters, La Comédie Humaine, of shallow moral judgements resulting in racial intolerance that is absent in those galloping television food safaris, but rises to the surface when confronted by our neighbours' culture or religious faith.

It is conceivable that some opinions expressed herein may be found unacceptable to some readers. But as long as any minority group can be used as a scapegoat for other people's social or political gain no group is safe. The Talmud tells the story of three men in a boat.

One begins to drill a hole under his seat. His companions beg him to stop. He responds: 'I am drilling the hole under my seat, why should you worry?' The moral being: We are all in the same boat.

Franz Kempf, September 2010

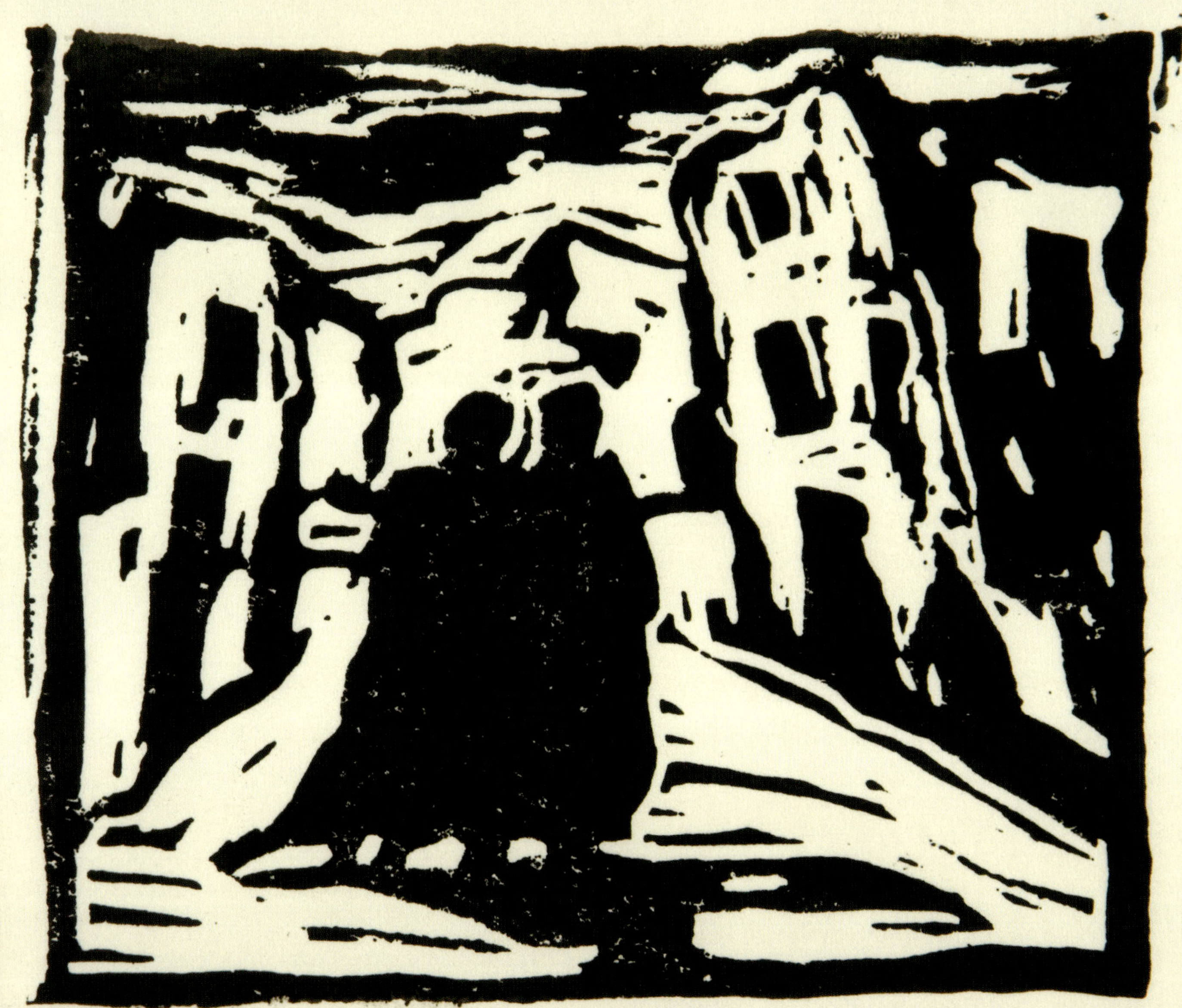

Flight Kempf

Flight

I do not see the prints as illustrations to text, but as symbolical, the expression of a feeling for the totality of a threatened world. They are concerned with the distressing state of our times.

Have they an existence apart from the printed page? Yes, but if I think of the great books of the fifteenth and sixteenth centuries, and the relationship that existed between the text and illustrations, I would like to see something of that harmony with these works, given the right typeface and design. These images in the widest sense are an embellishment to a text, a second voice, perhaps in the tradition of Der Sturm and Die Aktion. To quote (the great German Expressionist) Kaethe Kollwitz on the significance and legitimacy of the prints: 'I have as an artist the right to extract from everything its content of feeling, to let it take effect on me and to express it outwardly.'

We are all conditioned by the past and influences, perhaps none more so than the artist. An interviewer once asked Frank Auerbach which artists had influenced him, and got a list of more than fifty names. I cannot compete with Auerbach but there have been many: with some one sees the affinity, with others it is not so apparent. Robert Hughes has said that the sign of an educated artist is the ability to get something out of other art that has nothing overtly to do with that artist's own work. That something is the sense of quality, of eloquence and precision within the matrix of a different style, epoch and idea.

Dead Man Walking

As I view video clips of patrols moving
across a virtual minefield, laden with gear,
many not to return, others traumatised
to return with neurological disorders;
they appear as dead men slowly walking.

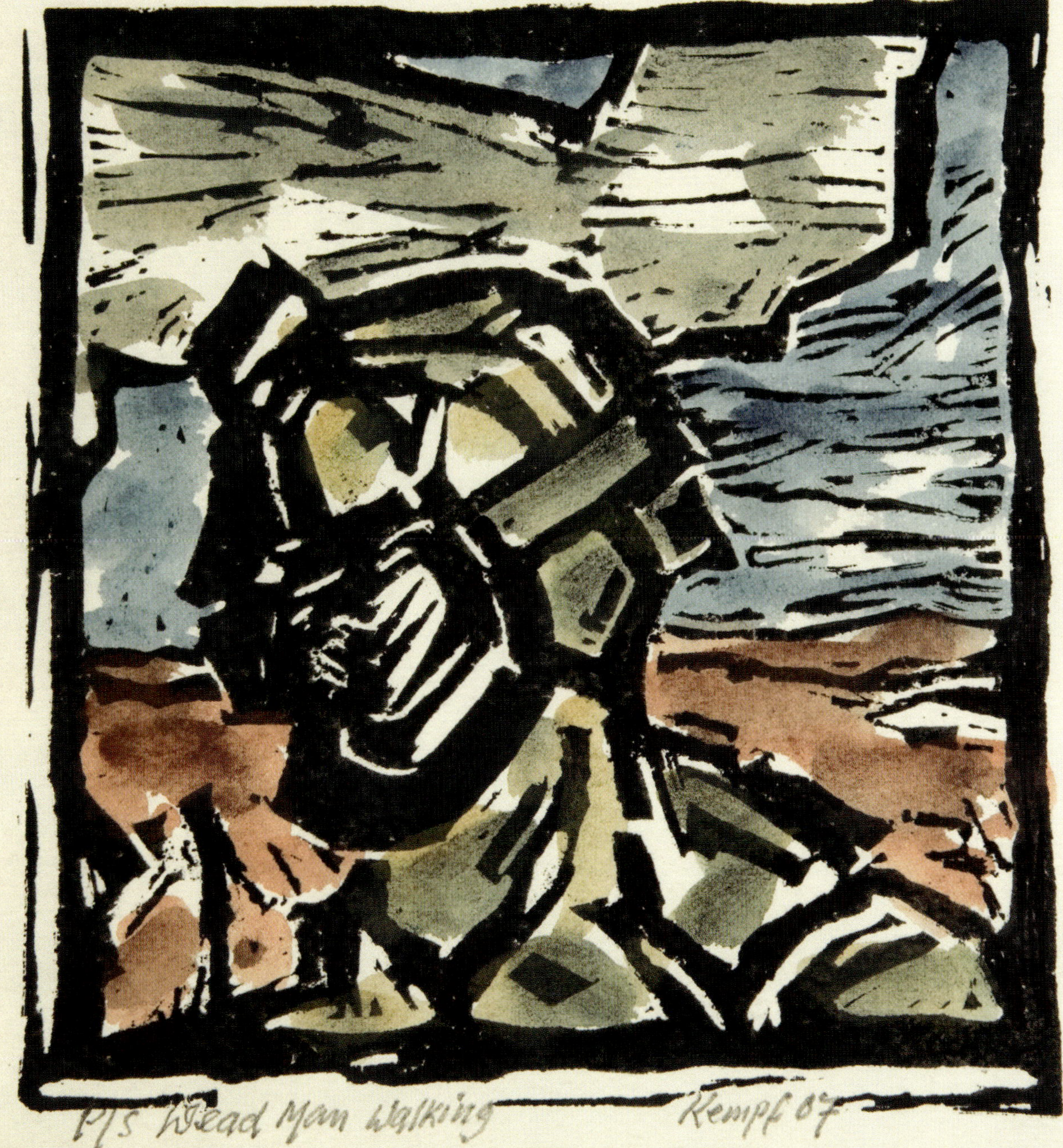
1/5 Dead Man Walking
Kempf 07

In the beginning was the word

'And the word was God'. After centuries of conflict, murder and torture, man's inhumanity to man is a crime no matter how we interpret biblical text.

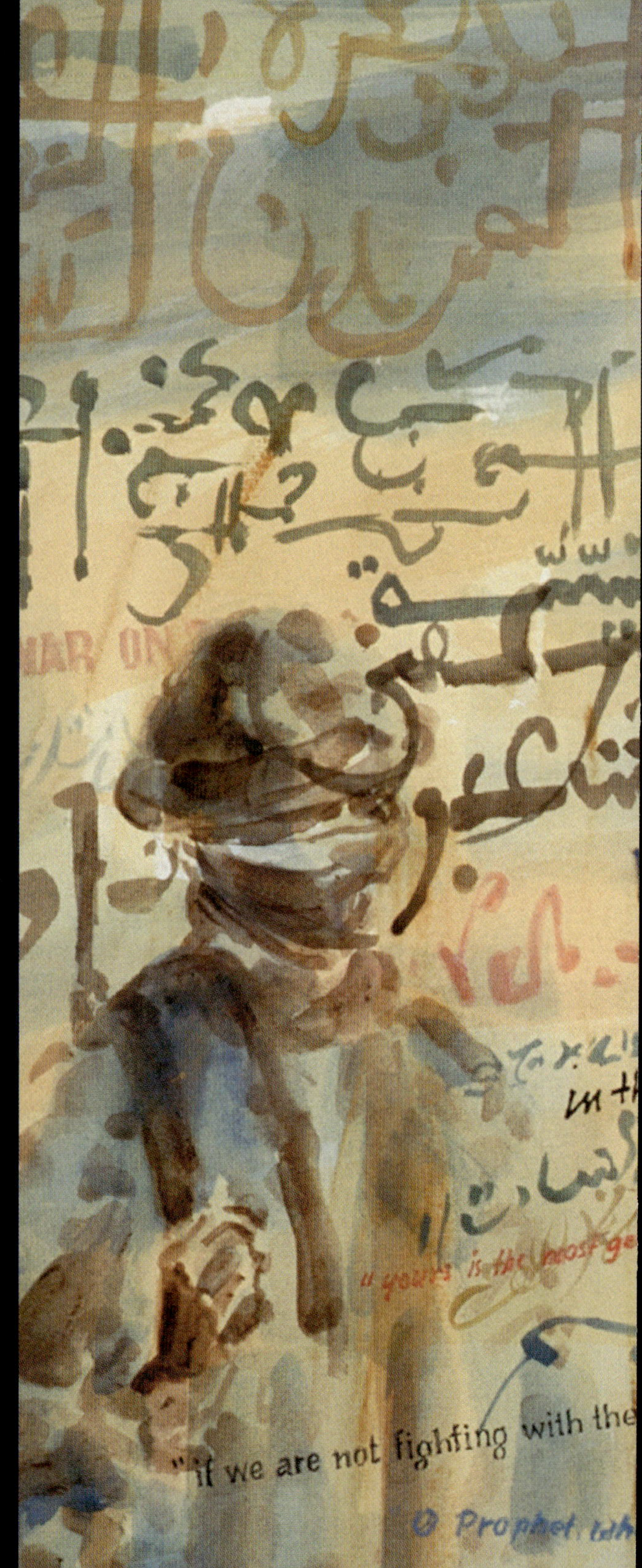

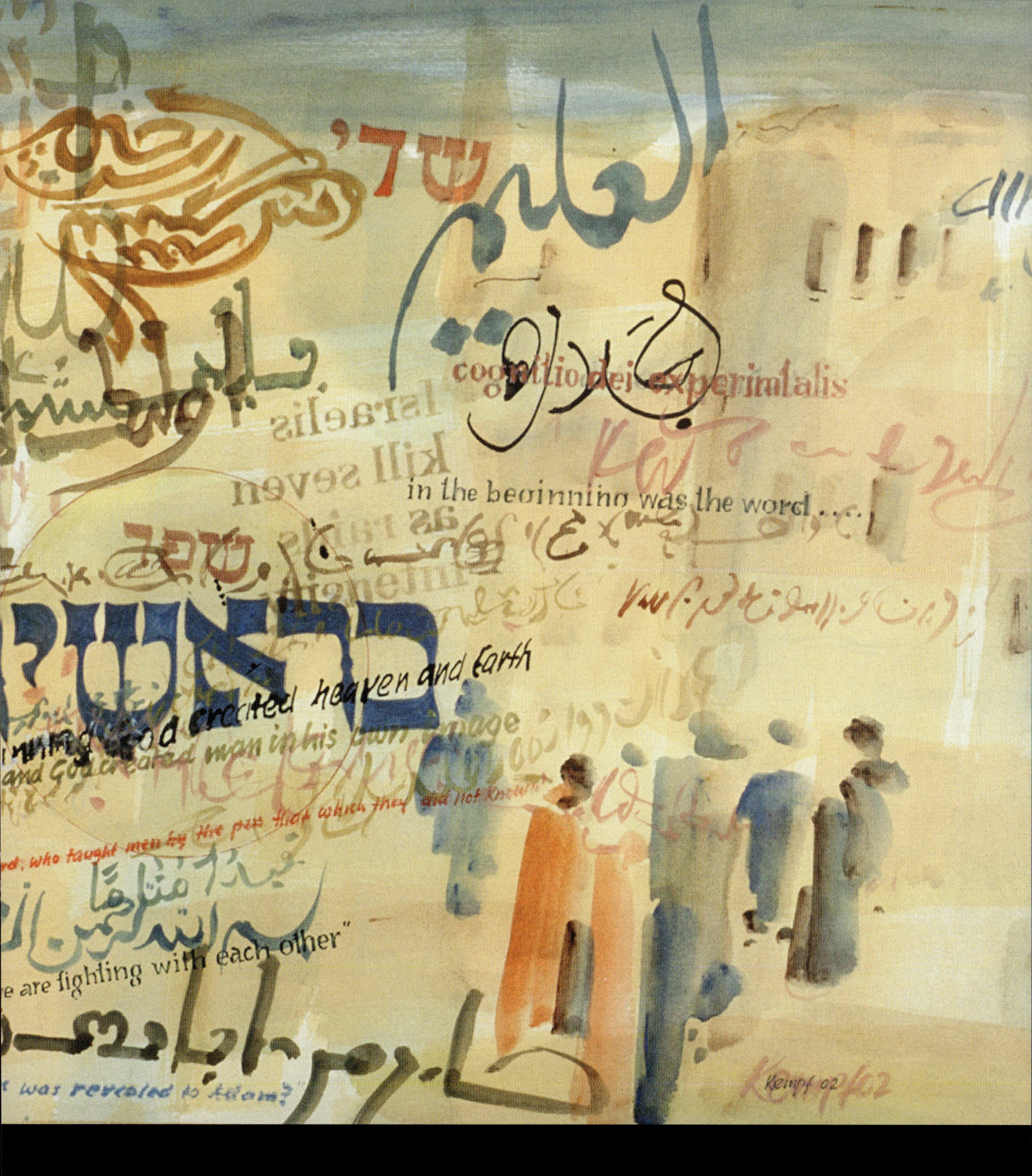
in the beginning was the word....
heaven and earth
e are fighting with each other"
Kempf 02

The Mother

Amongst the prints that I treasure is Kalwitz's *Schlachtfeld* ('Battlefield'). Against the dark night sky a mother searches the field for her fallen son – an image of unutterable sadness. I have sought to show in my work that suffering and loss is universal.

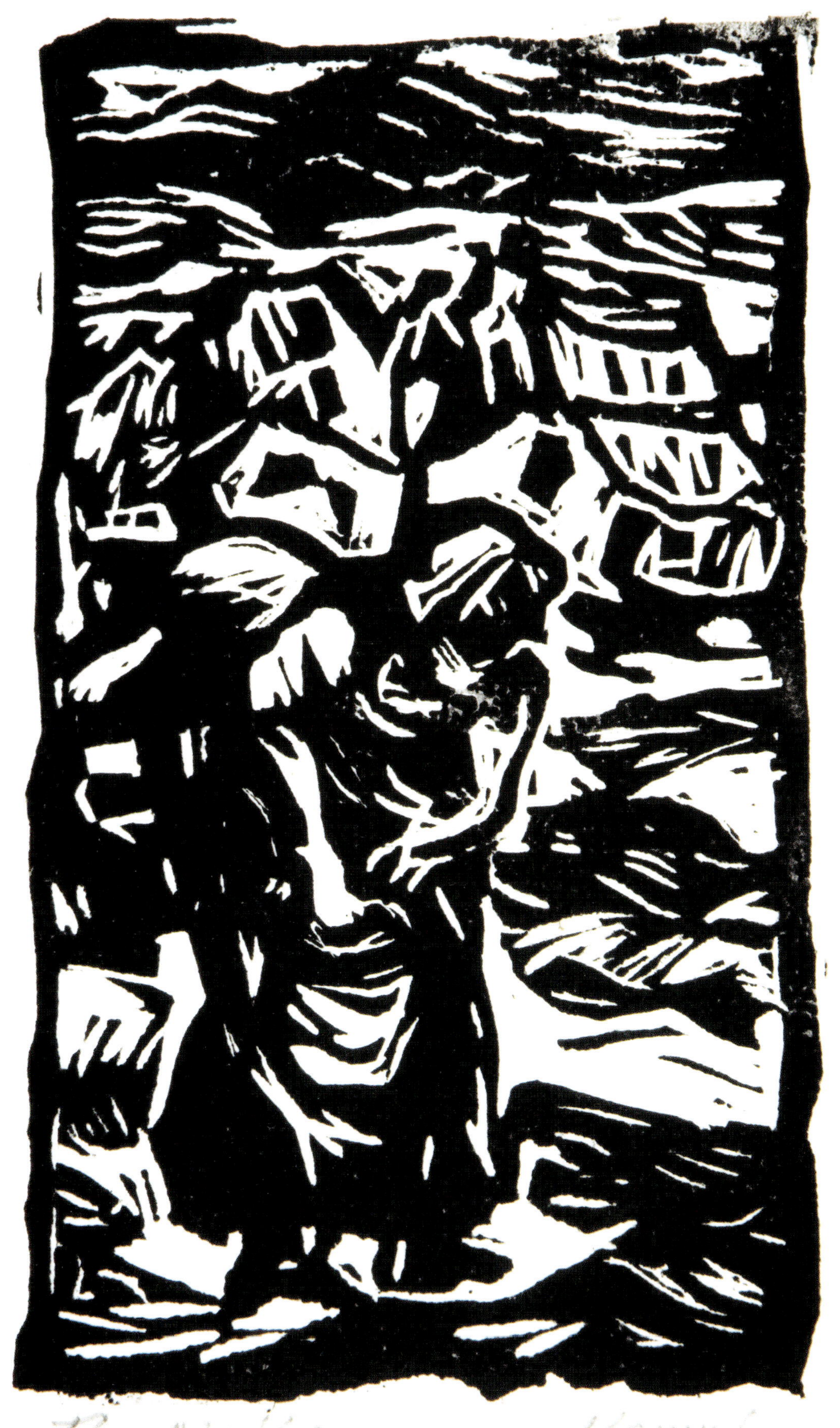

The Mother   Kempf

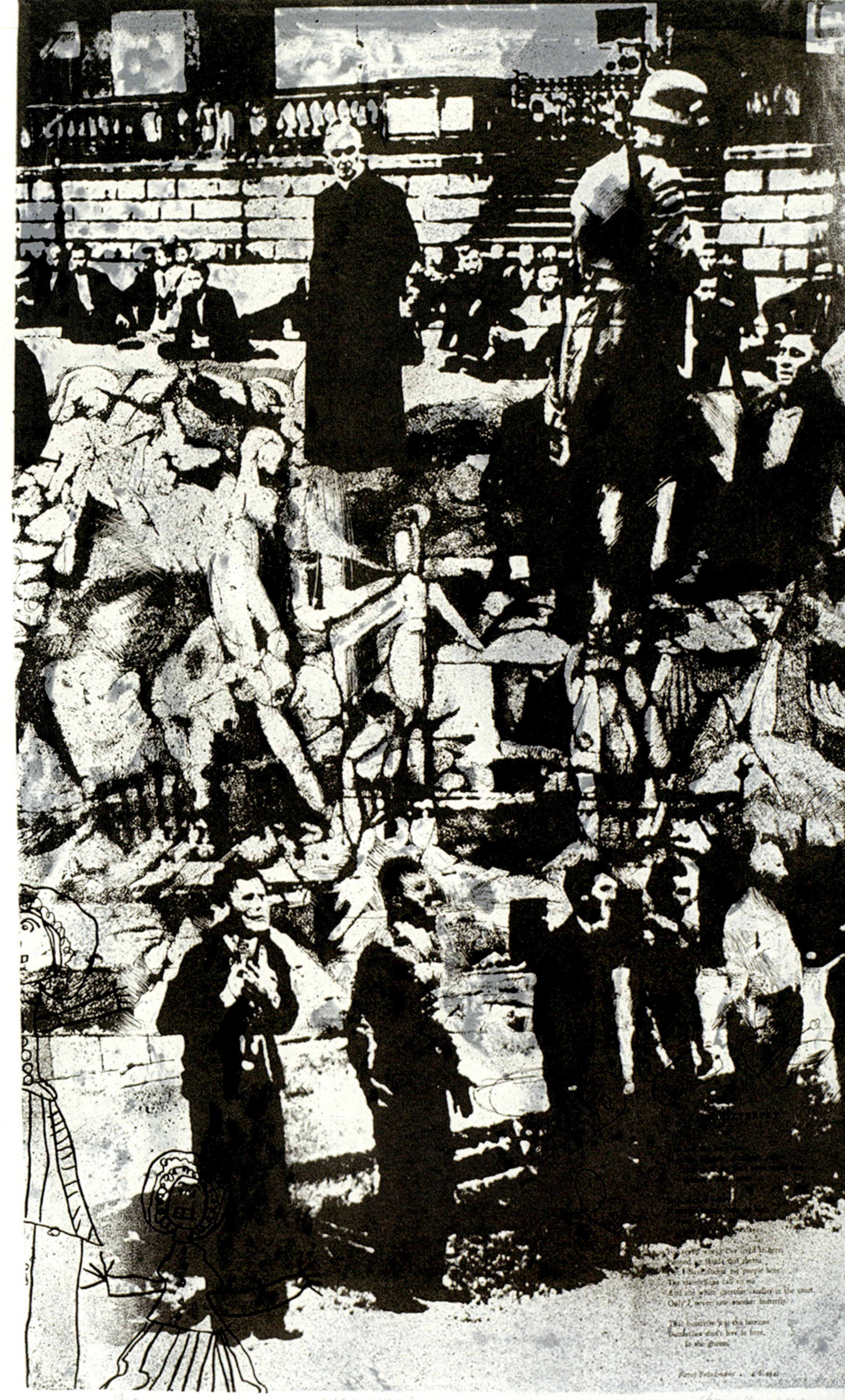
Memorial

A demonstration in Britain in 1979 resulted in the death of a teacher. Ironically, this was during the Year of the Child. These events focused my thoughts on our recent past, as I remember the words of Archbishop Dr William Temple, 'that anti-Semitism, like so many other national and international problems, though evil in itself, is symptomatic of still more fundamental disorders which threaten the very foundations of our civilisation.'

In such a situation, a responsibility rests on Jew and Christian alike.

By the juxtaposition of the child's drawing and verse from Theresienstadt against the oppressive form of the persecutors, I wish to emphasize the enormity of their crime and at the same time relate the work to the Year of the Child in an ongoing way. Fifteen thousand children under the age of 15 passed through Terezin; of these, around 100 returned. The central figure of the Priest, who was to become a prisoner in Auschwitz, is intended to be read as a symbol for those Christians who were persecuted for opposing National Socialism, and the clergymen, Franz Reinisch, Bernard Lichtenberg and Father Wachsmann, who were murdered.

In a sense, these prints are concerned with time, place and record. The memory of even these events can be influenced by time. What does not change are the records of those taken: they still live as moving symbols, as do the fragments and graffiti that express man's will to survive.

I have taken these elements and created a map in which the viewer is asked to chart his own journey.

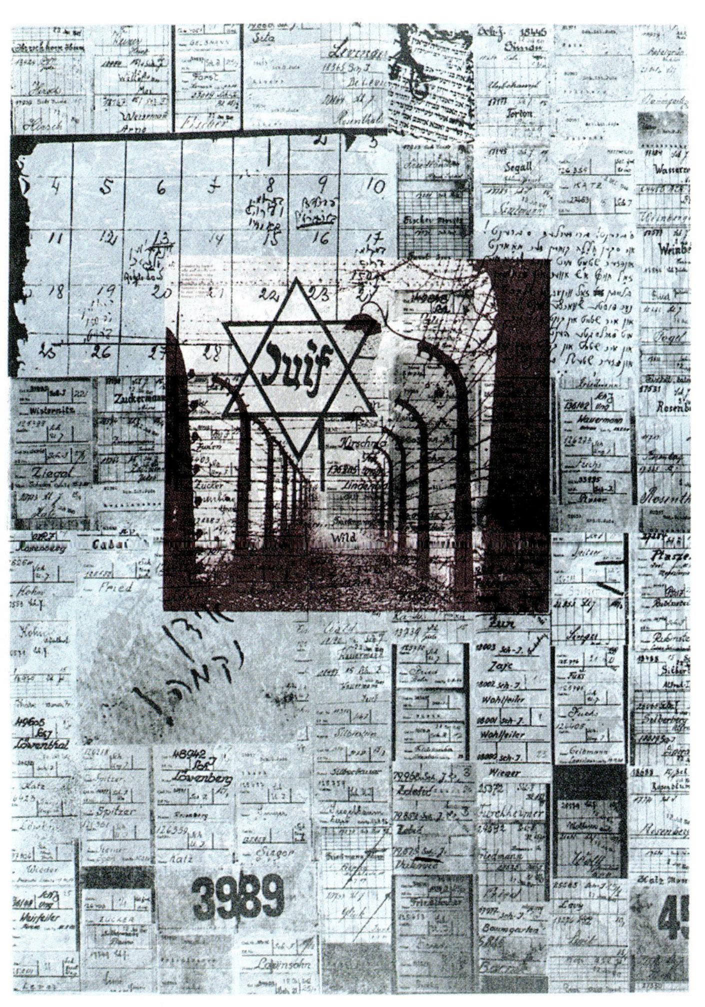
Juif
3989

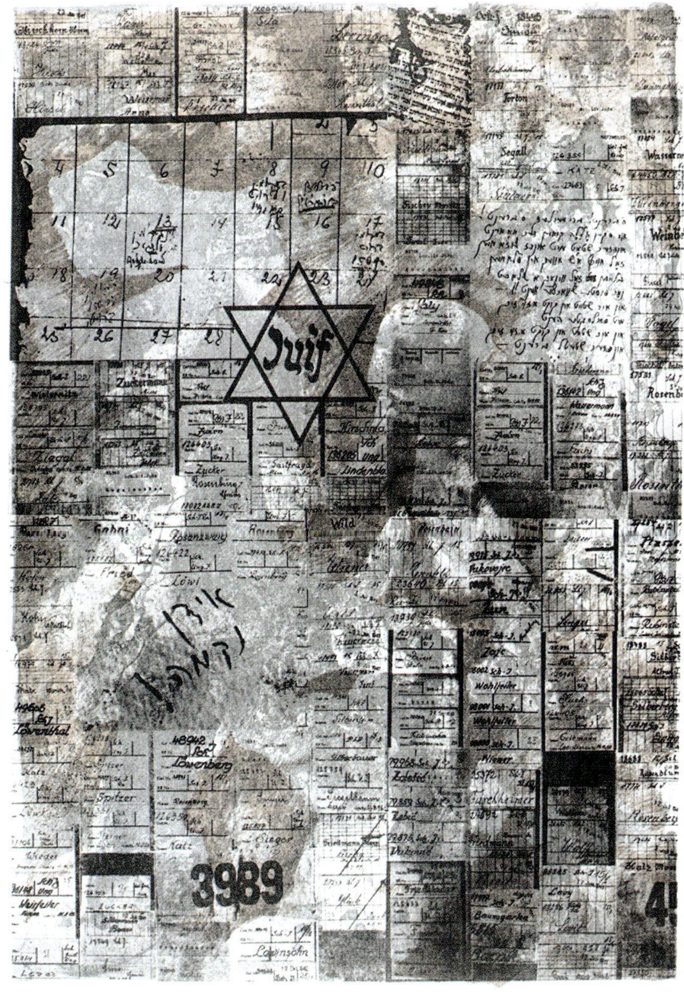
Juif
3989

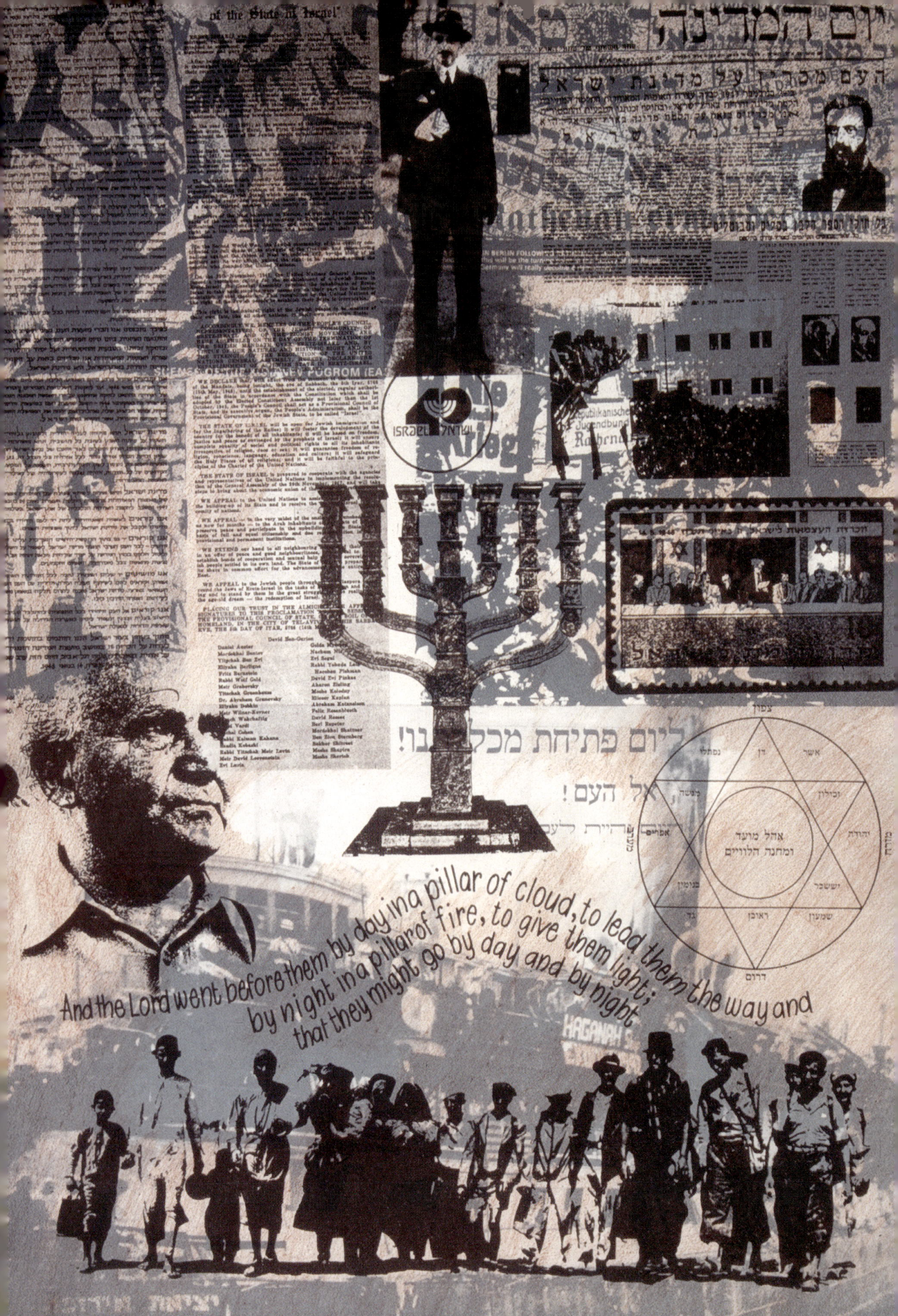

of the State of Israel
יום המדינה
ISRAEL
אל העם !
And the Lord went before them by day in a pillar of cloud, to lead them the way and
by night in a pillar of fire, to give them light;
that they might go by day and by night
HAGANAH

Tikvatenu/Our Hope

For one picture to encapsulate all that Israel or the 40th Anniversary means to every Jewish person is an impossible task.
I can only hope that my personal response to it strikes a chord that enables each viewer to reach a level of understanding.

I have selected images that are meaningful to me, were recurring events in our history, and therefore inseparable from the creation of the State.

The desecrated Torah Scrolls from the Kishinev pogroms can be seen as symbols for all pogroms and the Holocaust. The heading and the figures in the street are from the Berliner Tageblatt, following the murder of Walter Rathenau when a million Jews and unuionists attended his funderal. This and the banner headings from now defunct Yiddish Press illustrate the fragility of the Diaspora.

The dreams and visions of all those that held to the words of Ezekiel, 'When I shall have gathered the House of Israel from the peoples among whom they were scattered', are represented by the Magin David and the Menorah. Also included is a family group of the Ahad'Ha'am, whom I have long admired for his work in the national resurrection of the country, the Hebrew University and the quality of his views on Jewish existence.

The title of the lithograph is 'Tikvatenu/Our Hope'. This is deliberately linked to our National Anthem. It was a poem written in 1878 by Naphtali Herz Imber to record the founding of Peth Tikuah. Sadly he died as an alcoholic in America. It expresses the timeless relevance of the title, link with the past and hope for the future.

The Outrageous

Rev. John Bachman (1790–1874), American Lutheran minister, social activist, naturalist and founder of Newberry College, writes, 'The war is no longer declared but contrived. The outrageous has become commonplace. So what has changed? We are now confronted by a disdain for diplomacy, and a reliance on military or paramilitary forces to settle disputes. With little concern for the innocent victims. Collateral damage?'

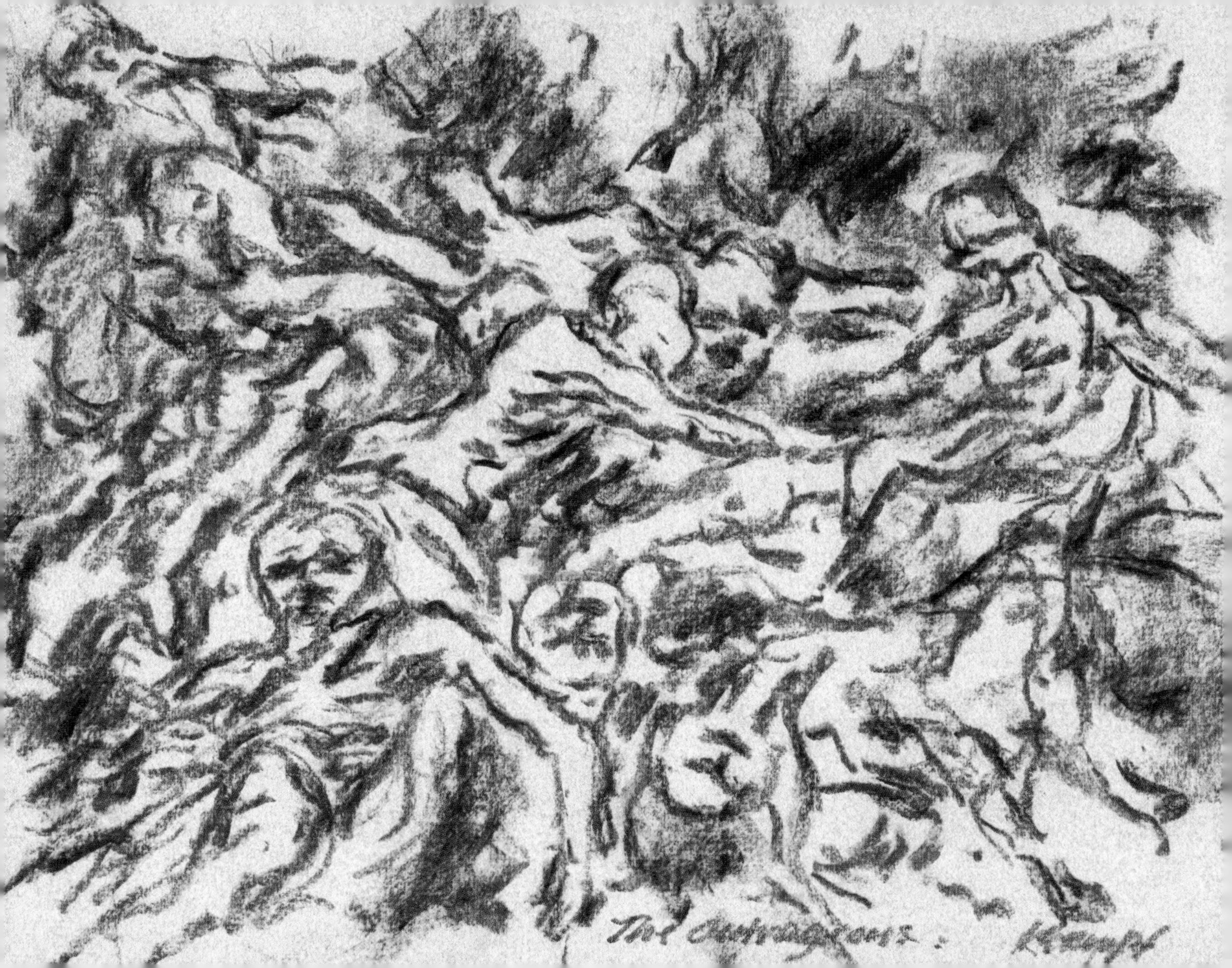

It May Not End Justly

It is a game,
I am dubious
It may not end
Justly.

– Johannes Bobrowski

Conflict does not always end justly. Peace becomes a prelude to the next war and more flag-draped caskets, more photo opportunities. Everything has its time. A time to love and a time of peace. We can forget a time of hate, and a time of war.

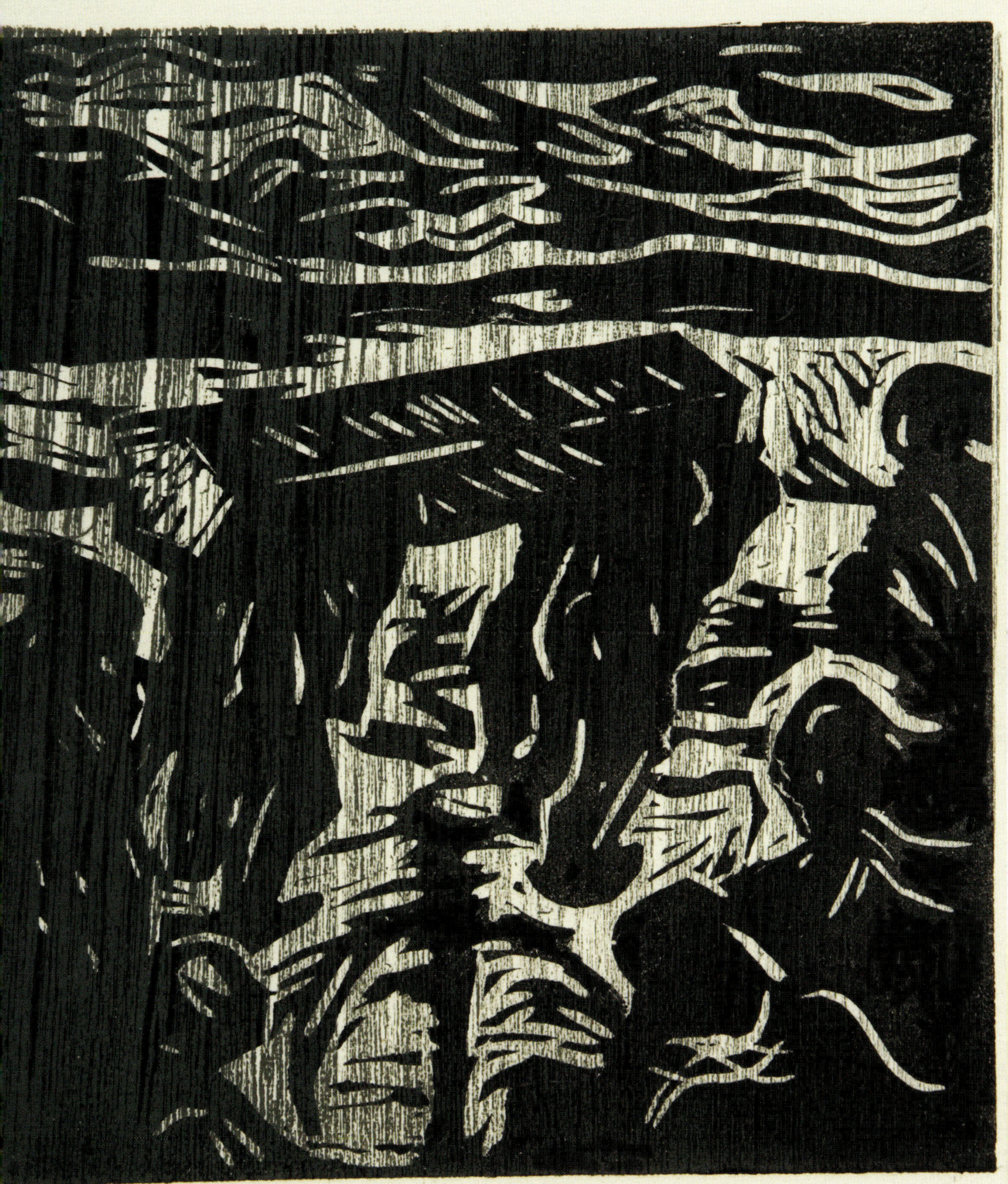

"It may not end justly" Kempf / 06

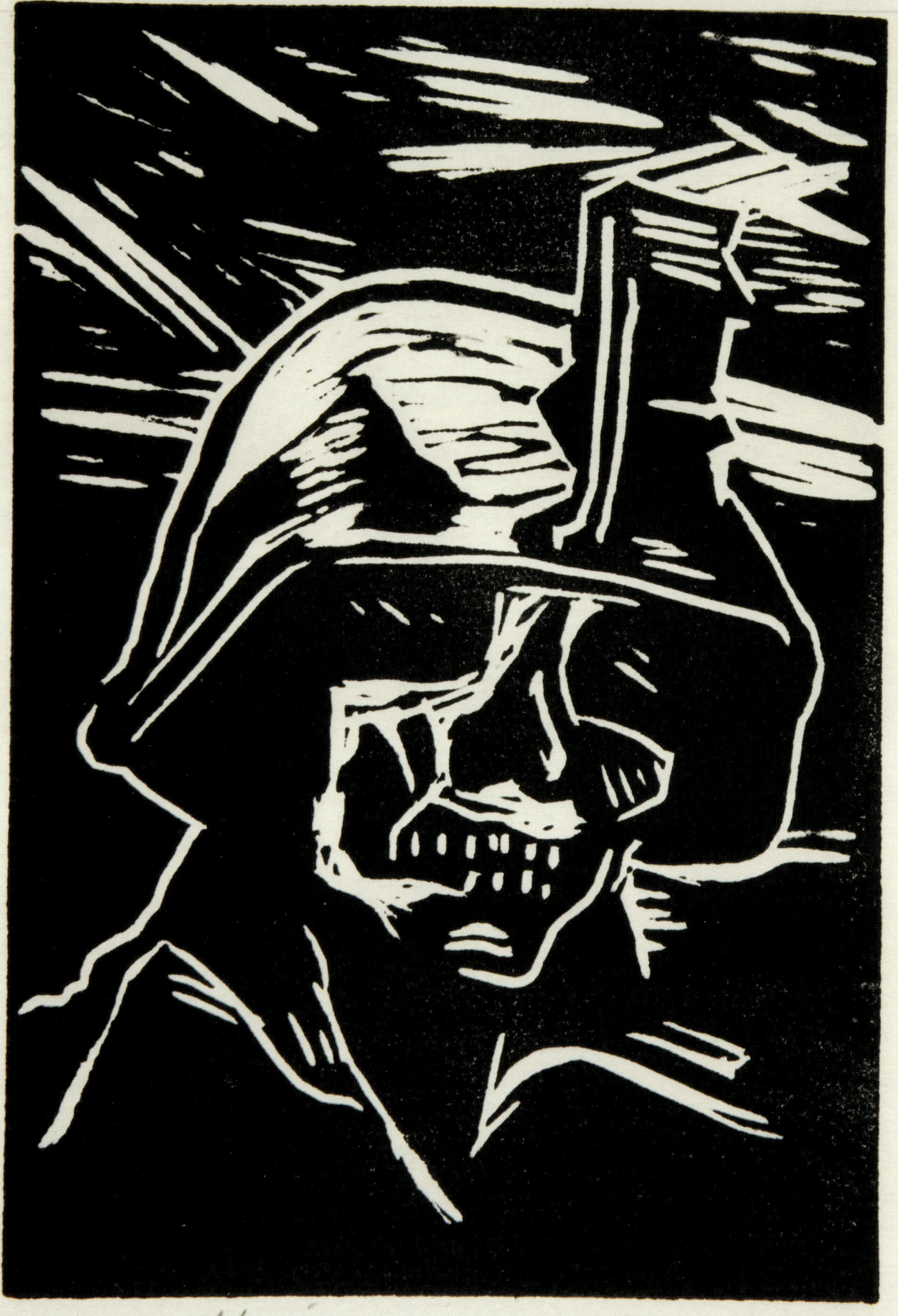

I bring you a new order Kemp/06

I Bring You a New Order

An aggressive American, unable to obtain a Waldorf salad ordered, demands the proprietor Basil Fawlty 'to get back in the kitchen and kick arse'. Whilst amusing, it is a reflection on British and American values. American compulsion to kick arse, when and wherever it feels the need, has left a trail of destruction, death and dysfunctional political systems in its wake! Time for dialogue in the kitchen?

Fear

November 2008: 2860 dead. 21,000 casualties, and that's only U.S. Forces. Iraqis? Who's counting? Does the text of country and western singer Toby Keith influence America's foreign policy, or does it reflect it? 'You'll be sorry that you messed with the U.S. of A./Cos we'll put a boot in your ass/ It's the American way.' Now there's a worry.

Lebanon, June 2006: 'Smart weapons appear unable to distinguish between military and civilian targets.' Give me a break.

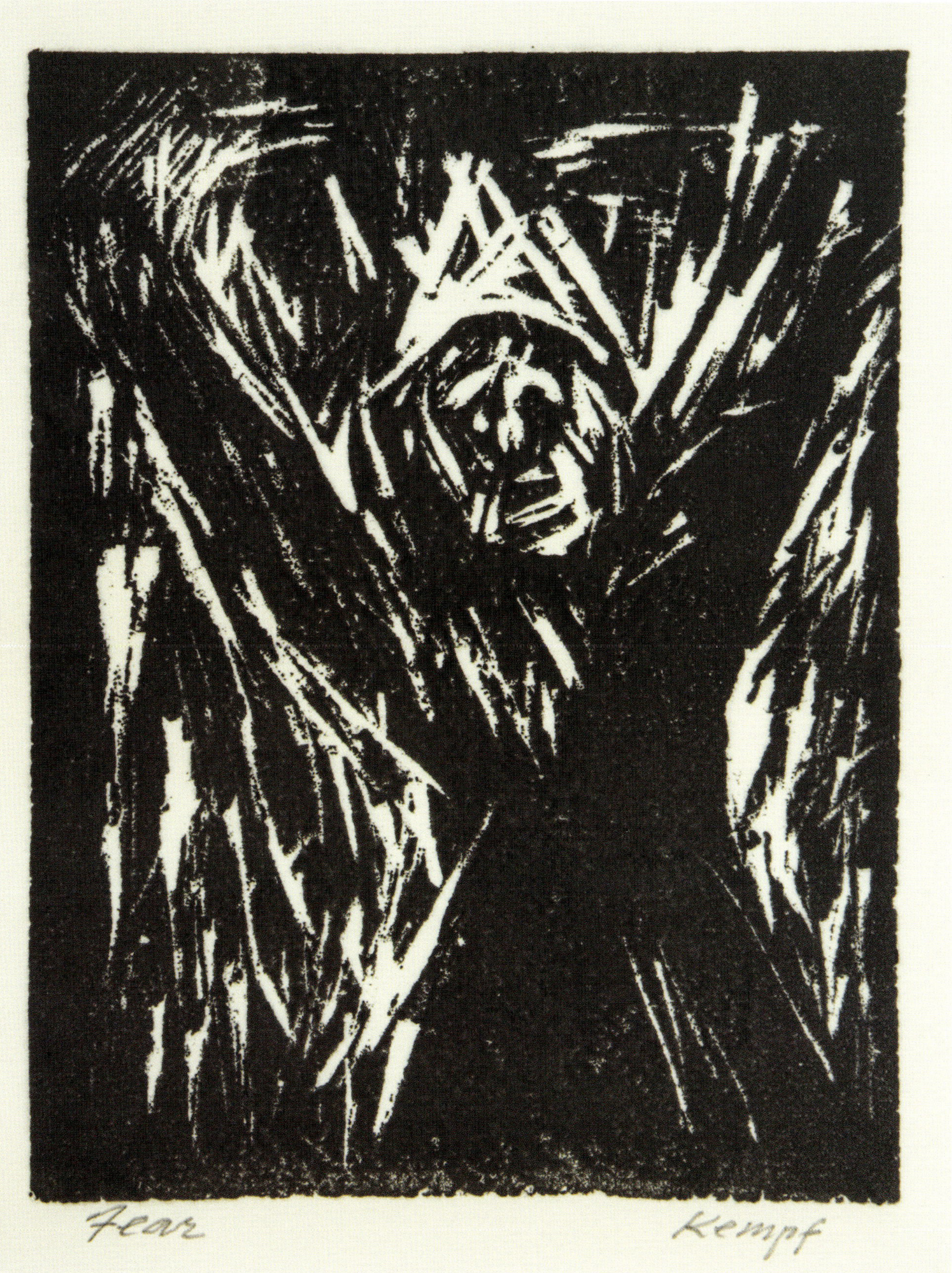
Fear
Kempf

31 March 2007 – 'Mission Accomplished', President Bush declares, the end of major combat operations in Iraq. We bring you a new order.

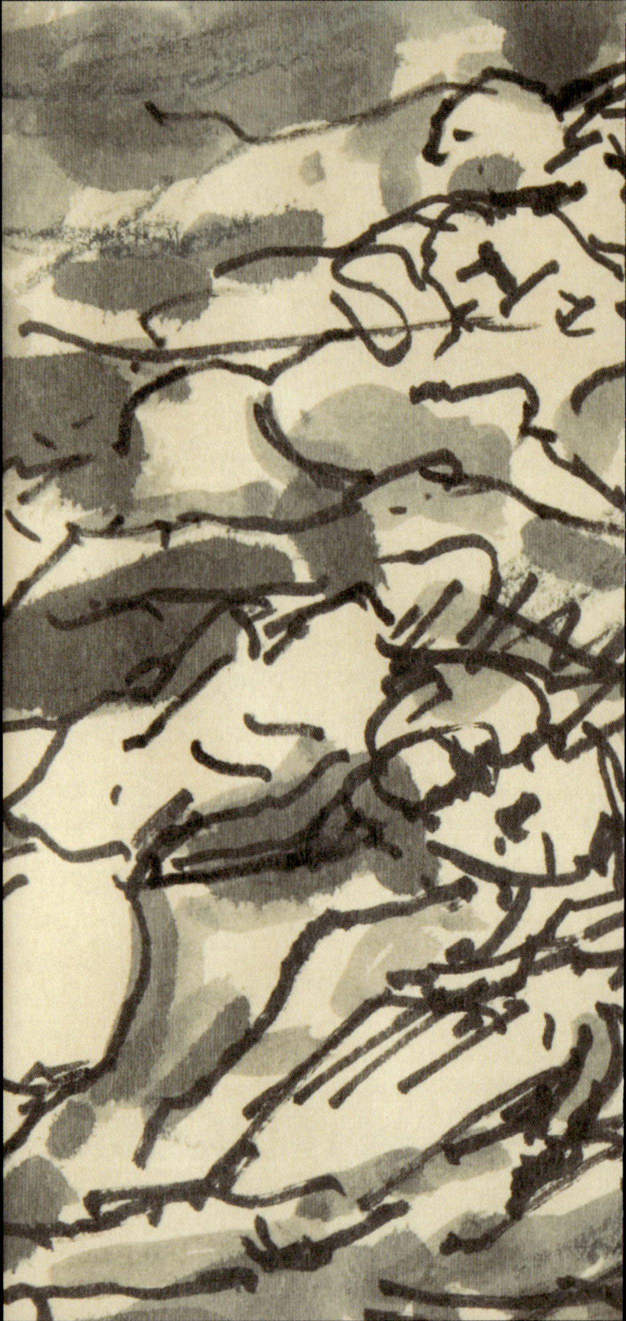

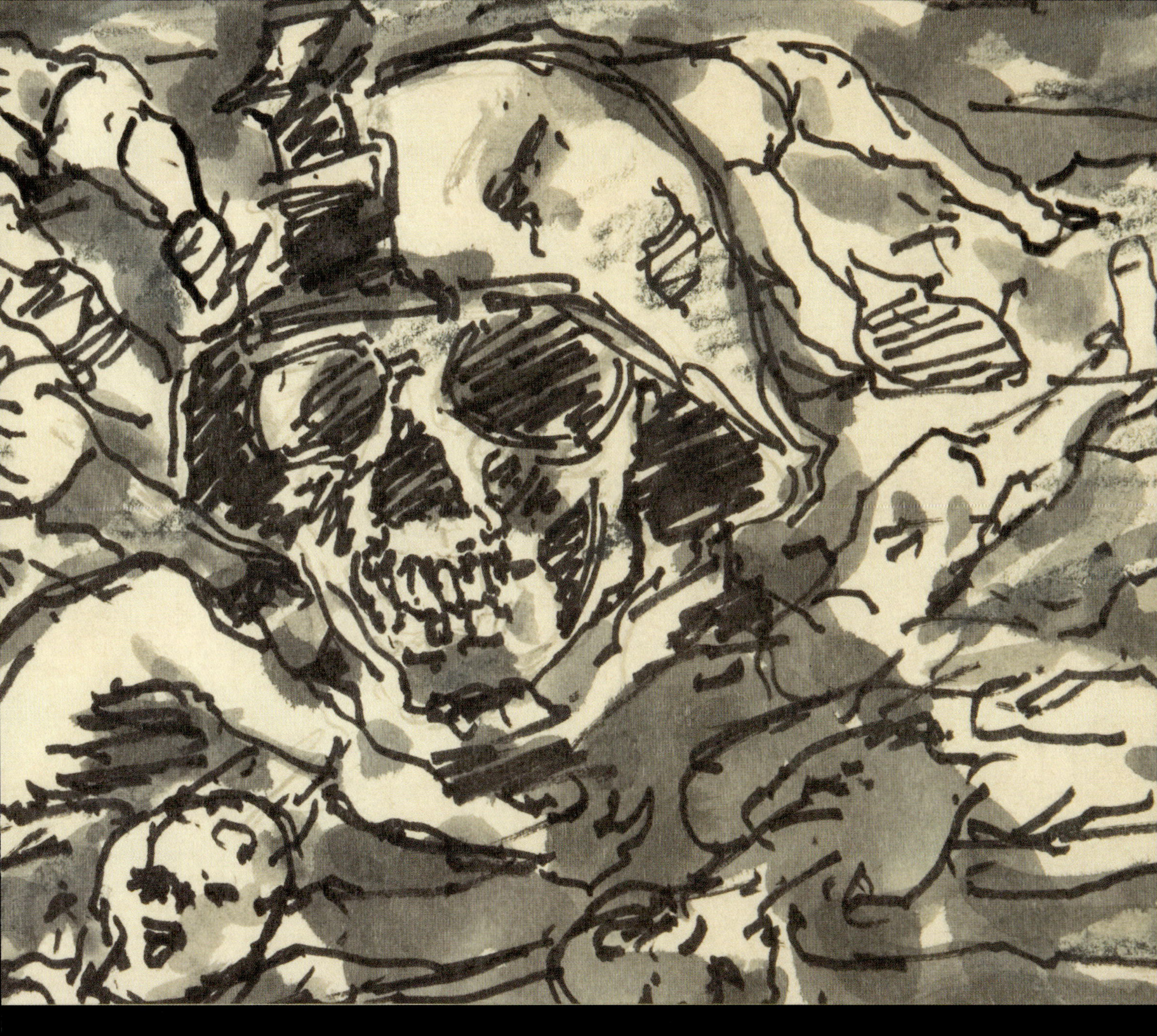

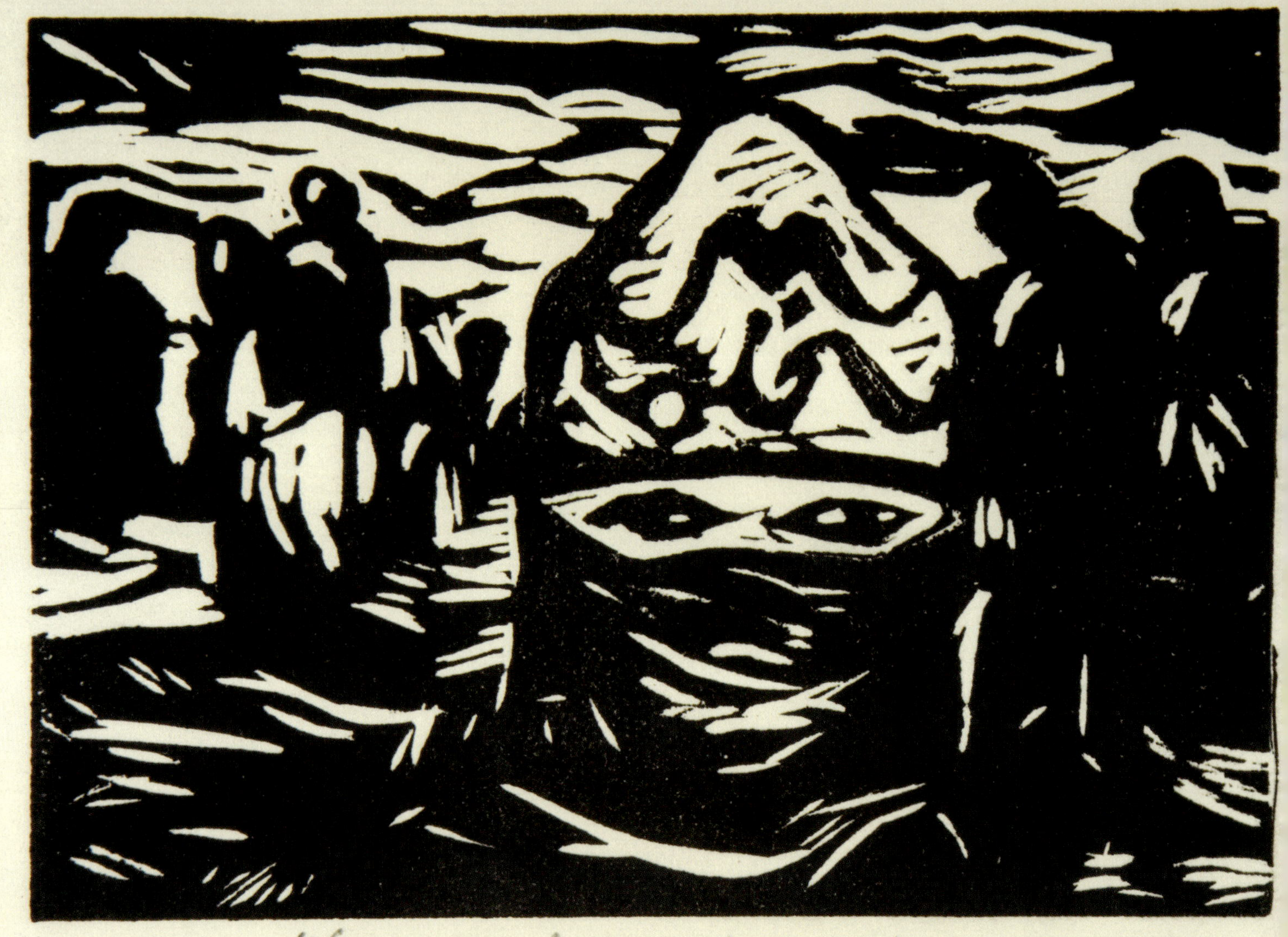

War is no longer declared.... Kempf 06

War is No Longer Declared

Fast forward to the lies and fabrications regarding weapons of mass destruction that led us into war with Iraq, when we all knew that it was just another colonial adventure and dependency on oil, the road to ruin for thousands of Iraqis and squandering the lives of American and Allied servicemen. Since the end of World War 2, the U.S. has attempted to overthrow some 40 regimes, supporting many brutal dictators.

It is said: 'The fox barks not, when he would steal the lambs.'

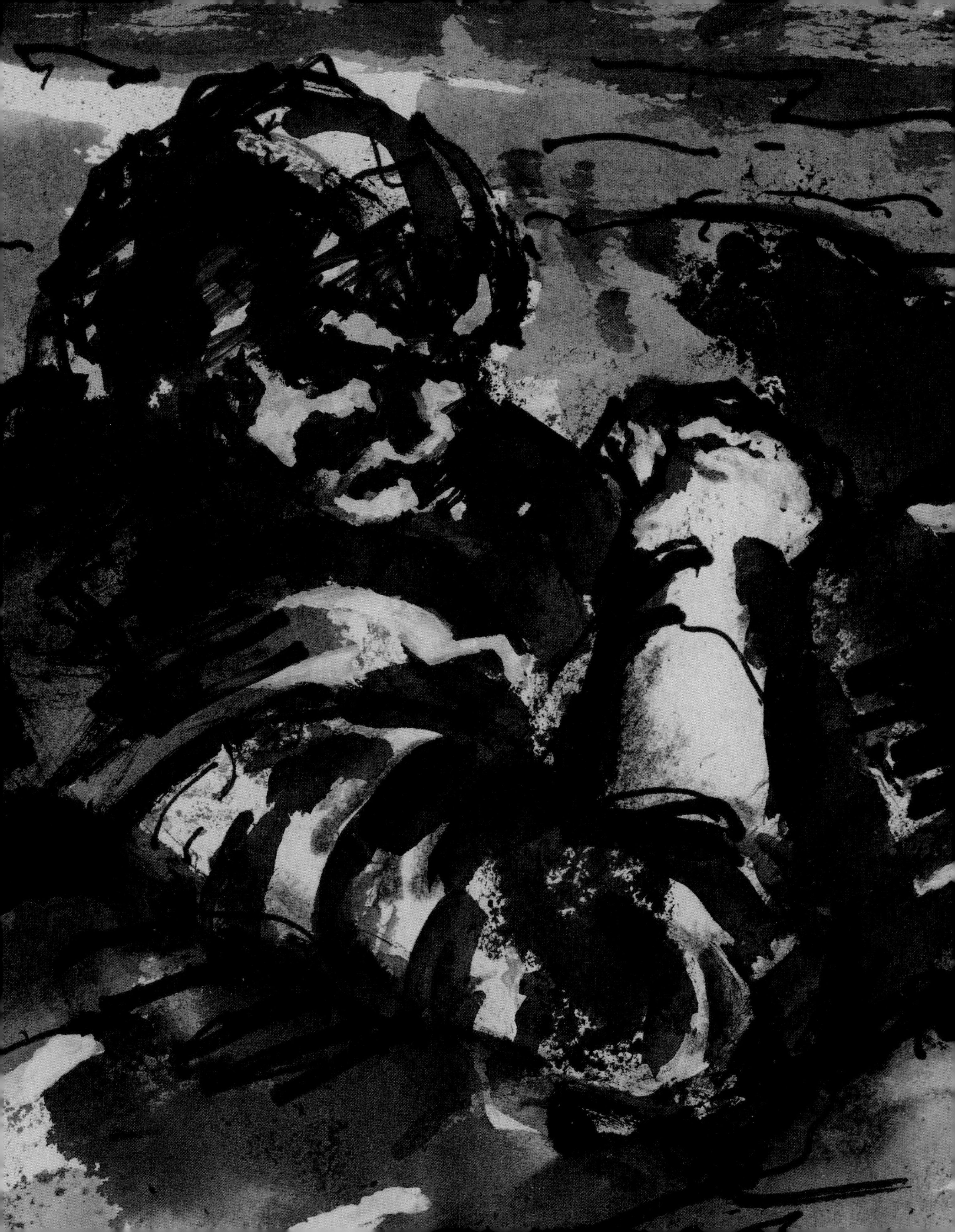

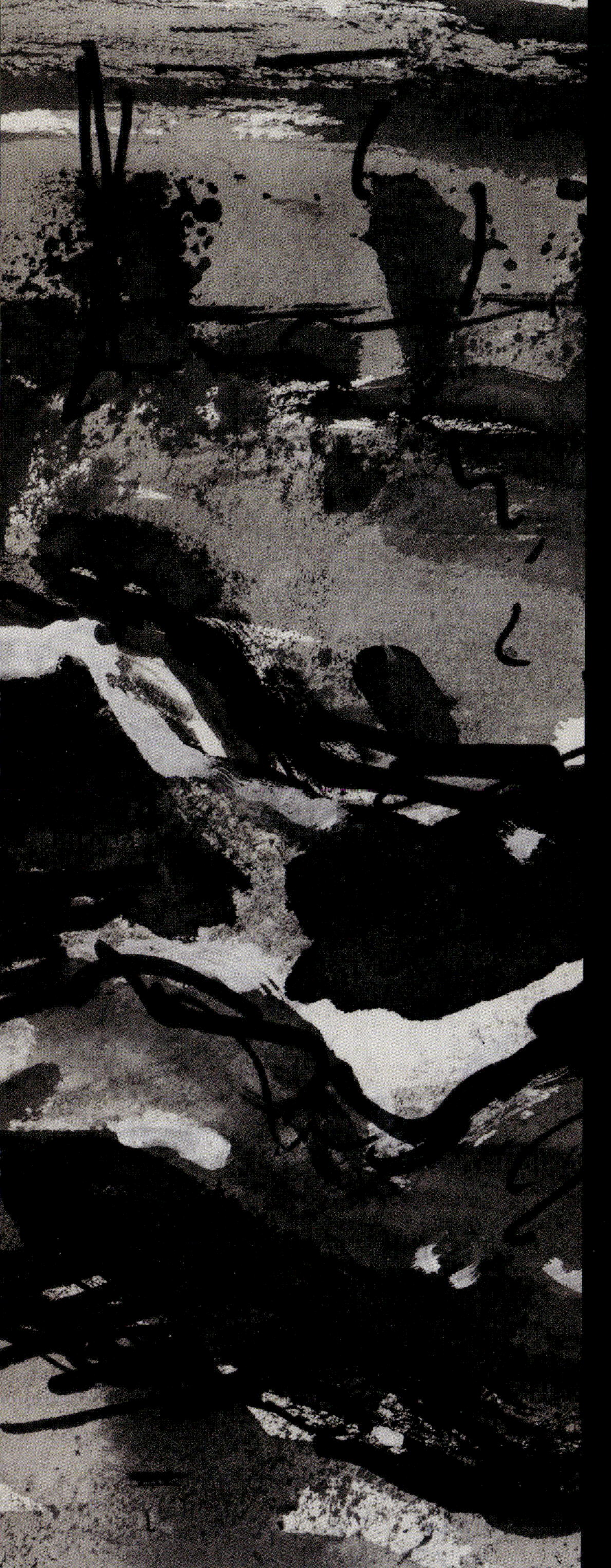

Into the Landscape

31 March 2007: As one reads of attempted and successful suicides amongst troops serving in Iraq and the appalling loss of life of non combatants, all those who marched against America's invasion of that

country, and of Australia's involvement, are now vindicated in their actions. Bush and Howard will not have to wait for history to judge them morally corrupt. Now as Bush begins his tirades against Iran, his callous disregard for life and cavalier attitude reminds one of Field Marshal Haig's comment when 19,000 men died during the first offensive on the Somme in 1916: 'I do not consider the casualties excessive.'

Perhaps Dresden, Hiroshima and the Holocaust were also not excessive now that we refer to our losses as collateral damage. No problems mate!

Lebanon

Lebanon, 2006: Creates another theatre of the absurd. An obscene crew of bit players having laid waste, will ultimately leave the stage wallowing in blood and tears. Now the Minister of Jerusalem Affairs says the government must decide on a name for the war. The play's the thing?

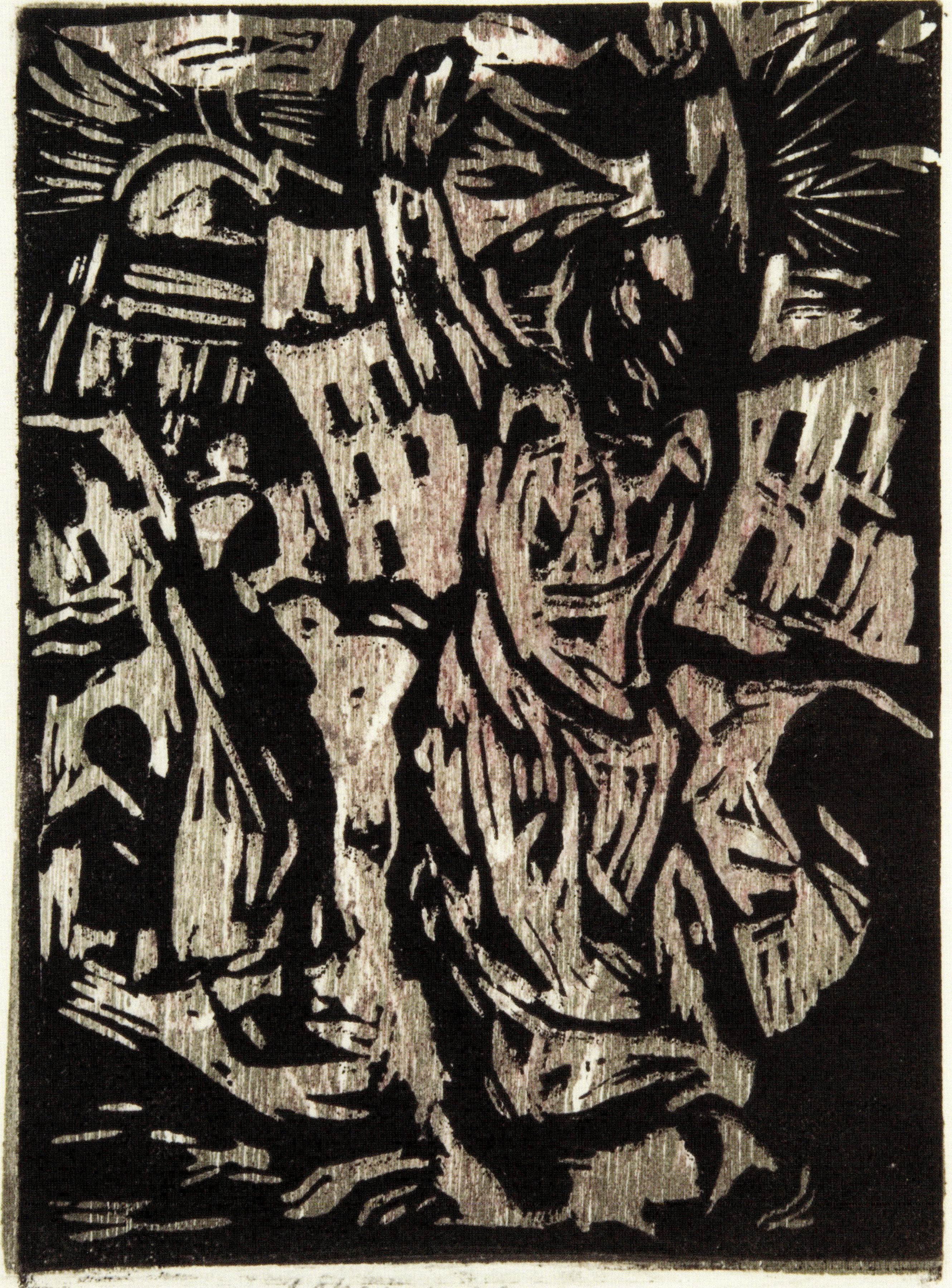

Lebanon 06 Kempf 06

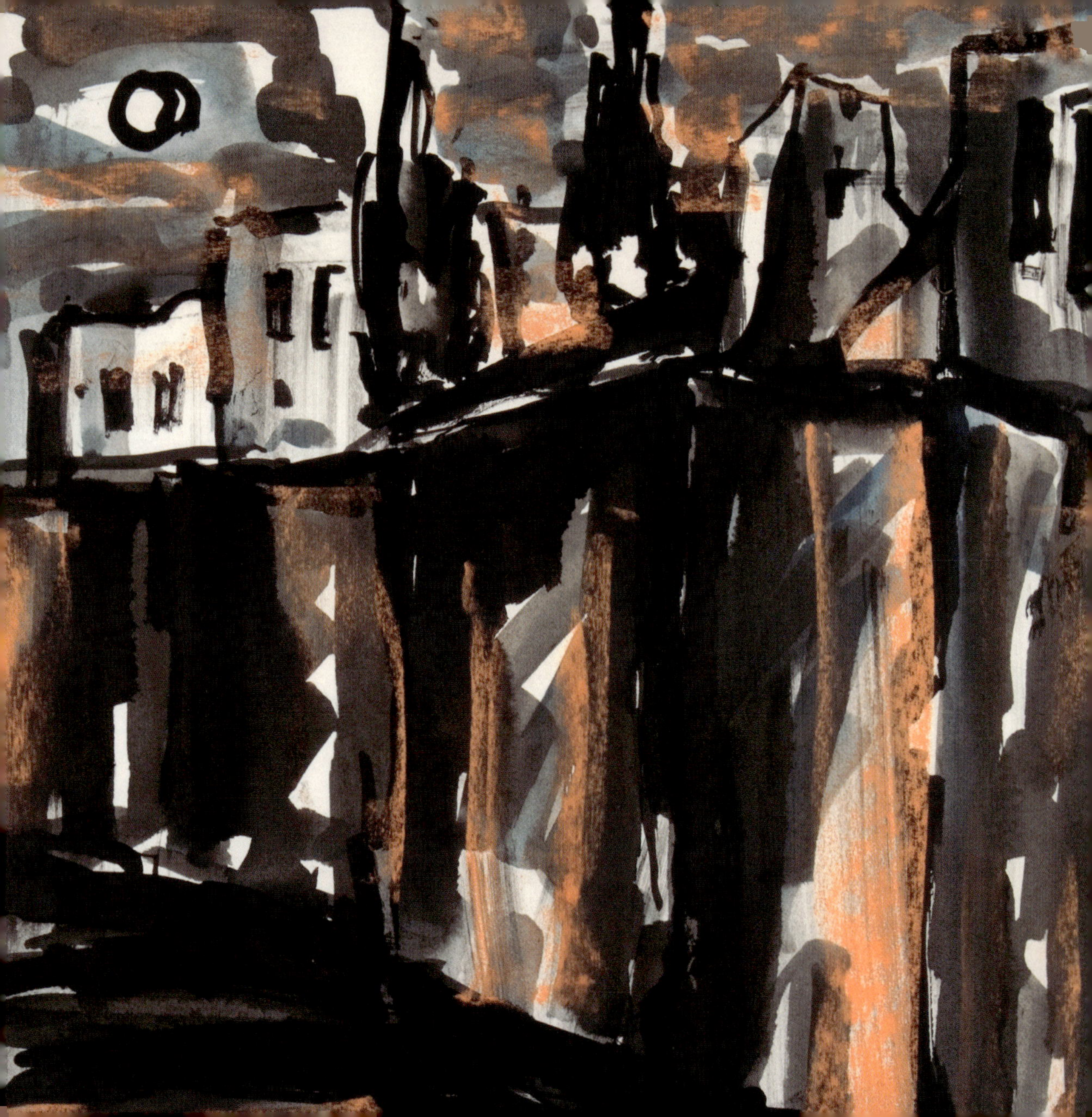

The Wall

Australia Day, 26 January 2008: What price the Palestinians making a hole in the wall? … It sometimes takes more than religion or politics to separate peoples … Palestinians today showing their initiative in blowing a hole in the wall and doing their shopping in Egypt, thus turning the streets of Rapha into a market place.

Israeli artists perhaps less explosive but equally creative have painted sections of the walls that separate them from their neighbours with scenes of what is on the other side. If one is driven to the wall the alternative is to go around, or through it.

Days of Masks and Riddles

10 July 2008: A few words re. the work. As we read and absorb the daily reports from the various theatres of conflict and suffering through the world, I see my options to either retreat into a negative state, or translate my response into visual terms. By working with prints, the direct physical activity becomes an expressive act in itself. The resultant image hopefully will convey a message to those who have not been completely debased by superficial and commercial images.

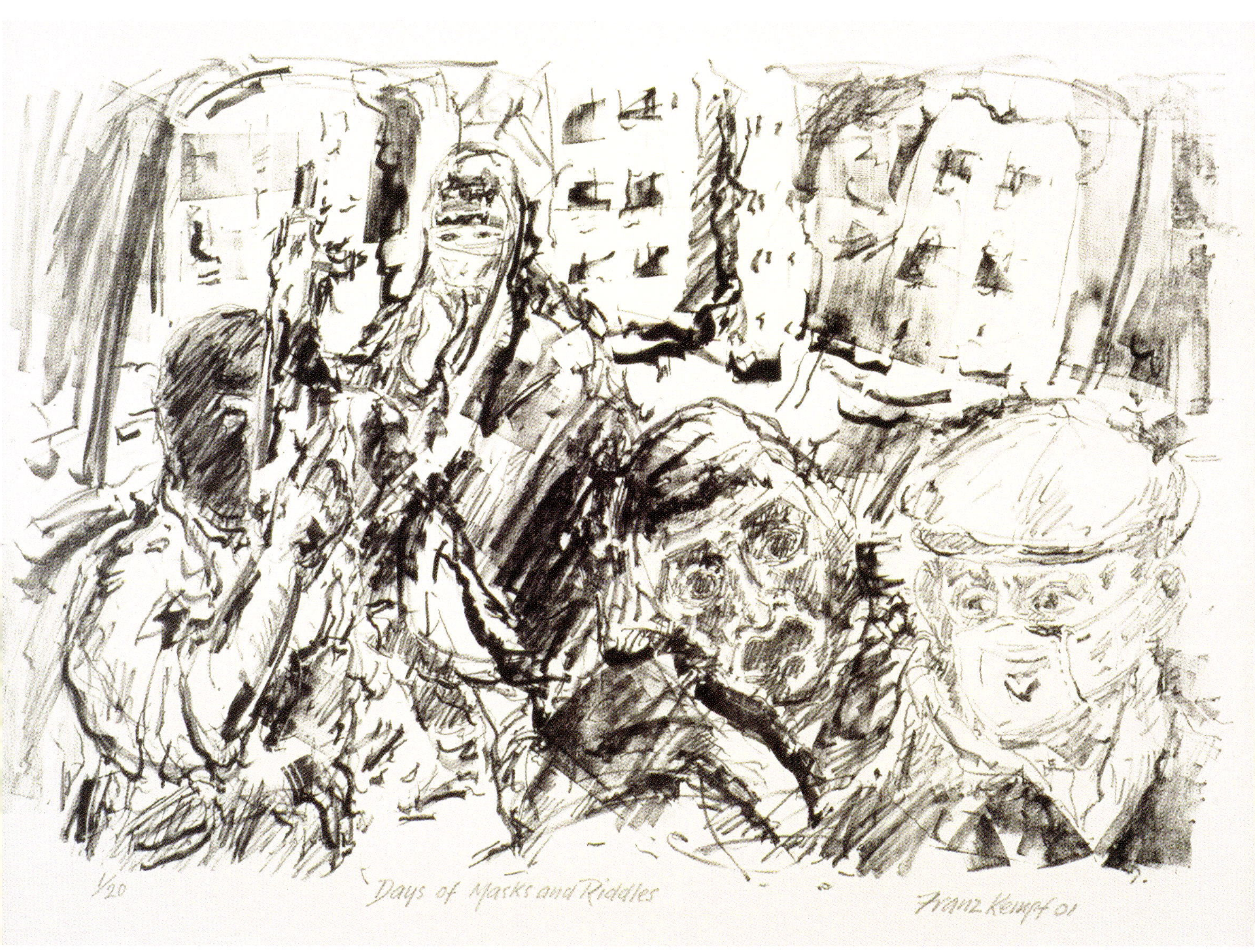
1/20
Days of Masks and Riddles
Franz Kempf 01

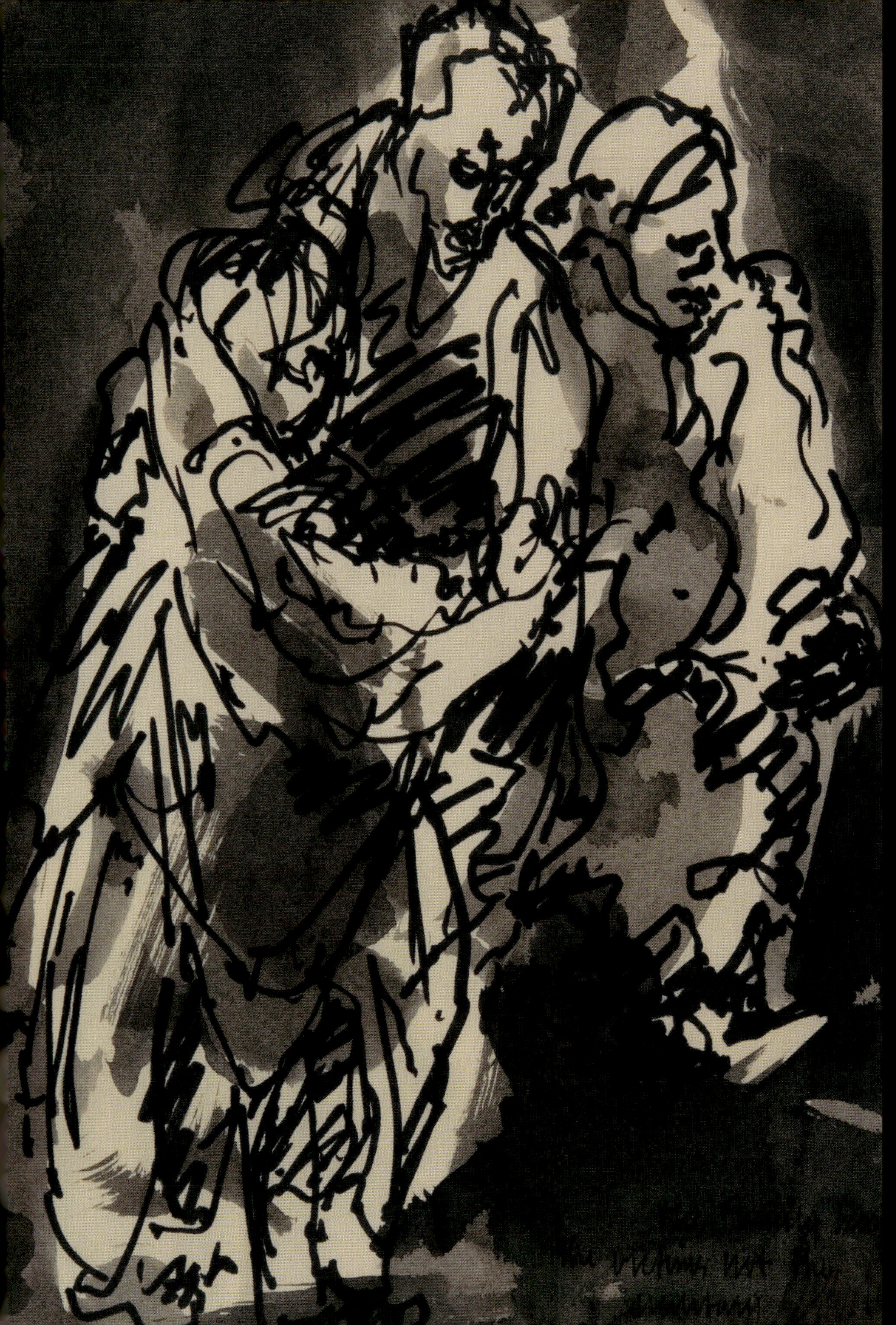

The Family Bosnia

January 2002: I live in a world that is both entrancing and disturbing. Feeling a modicum of social responsibility, I attempt to convey information about the human condition. At times this may be tranquil, expressive of an inner harmony, and often it will be expressive of disquiet, reflecting disillusion with the human condition and its abject state. The demands made by these voices is constant throughout my work.

We must respect the anguished human voice for we all live on this darkling planet threatened by ever growing madness.

By producing images I am able to chart a course for myself through this less than ideal and very intangible world. In such a world one becomes a sceptic or a heretic.

Confrontation

November 1993: Am I a Jewish artist – am I still a Jewish artist when not engaged in Jewish subject matter? Did Pisarro paint Jewish clouds? Is not Rembrandt's *The Jewish Bride,* one of the most tender and enduring Jewish paintings?

Why does one concern oneself with these questions, as well as mindless reviews, or much elementary rhetoric that passes for information? Perhaps because the response is so often dependent on who frames the question and how distorted that response may subsequently become.

When I put these questions to myself it is because of a dilemma I am sure I do not face alone: what is my contribution to society, does this world we have inherited require more paintings?

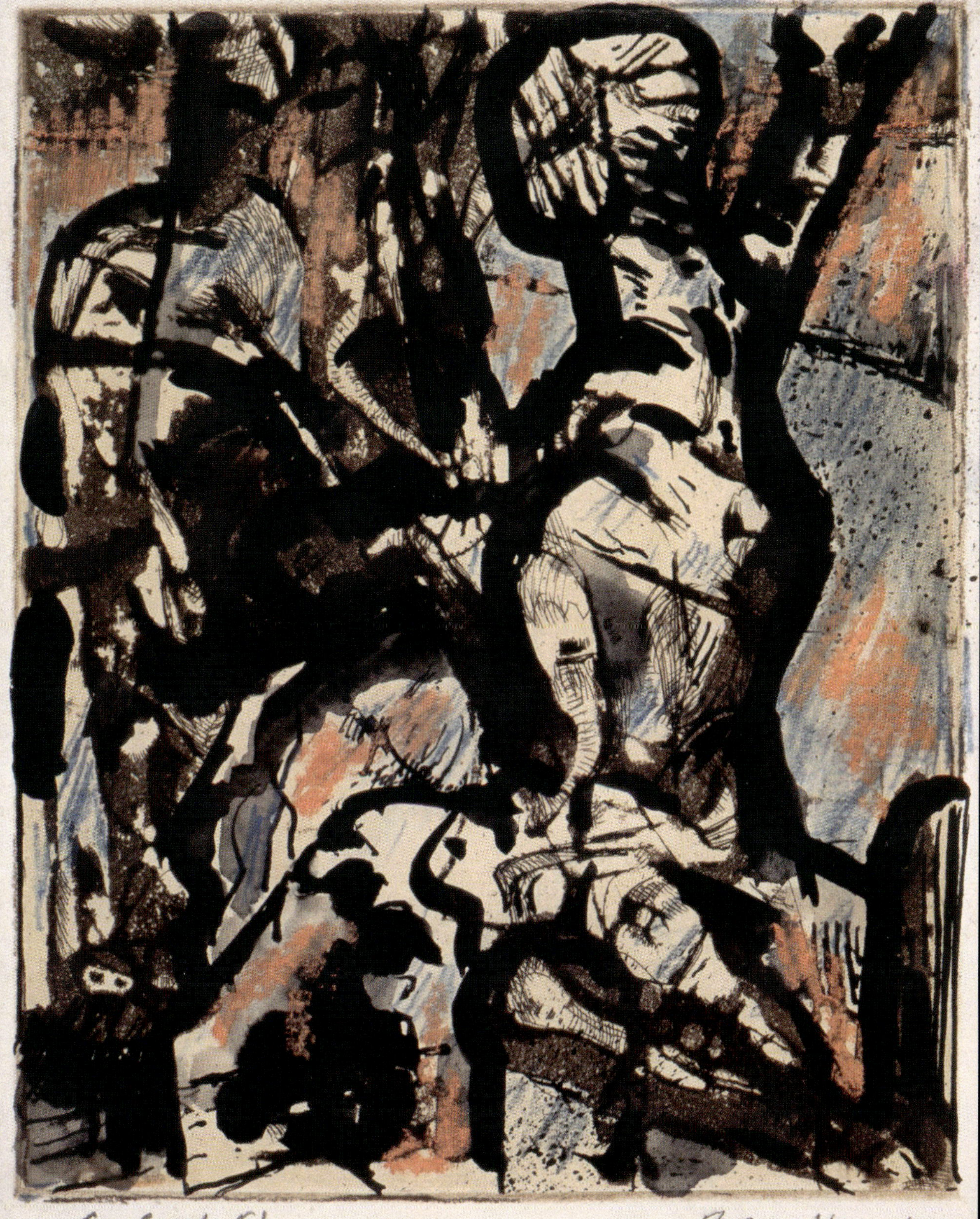
Confrontation
Franz Kempf 98

And Still it Goes On

February 2007: Should we be surprised at the release of the so-called 'Family Jewels' by the American Intelligence service (in 2007, the CIA finally released previously secret files listing 25 years of Agency misdeeds) and the revelations of their misdirected energy and bungling? One would be naïve indeed to believe that such an organisation was about to change direction despite media criticism.

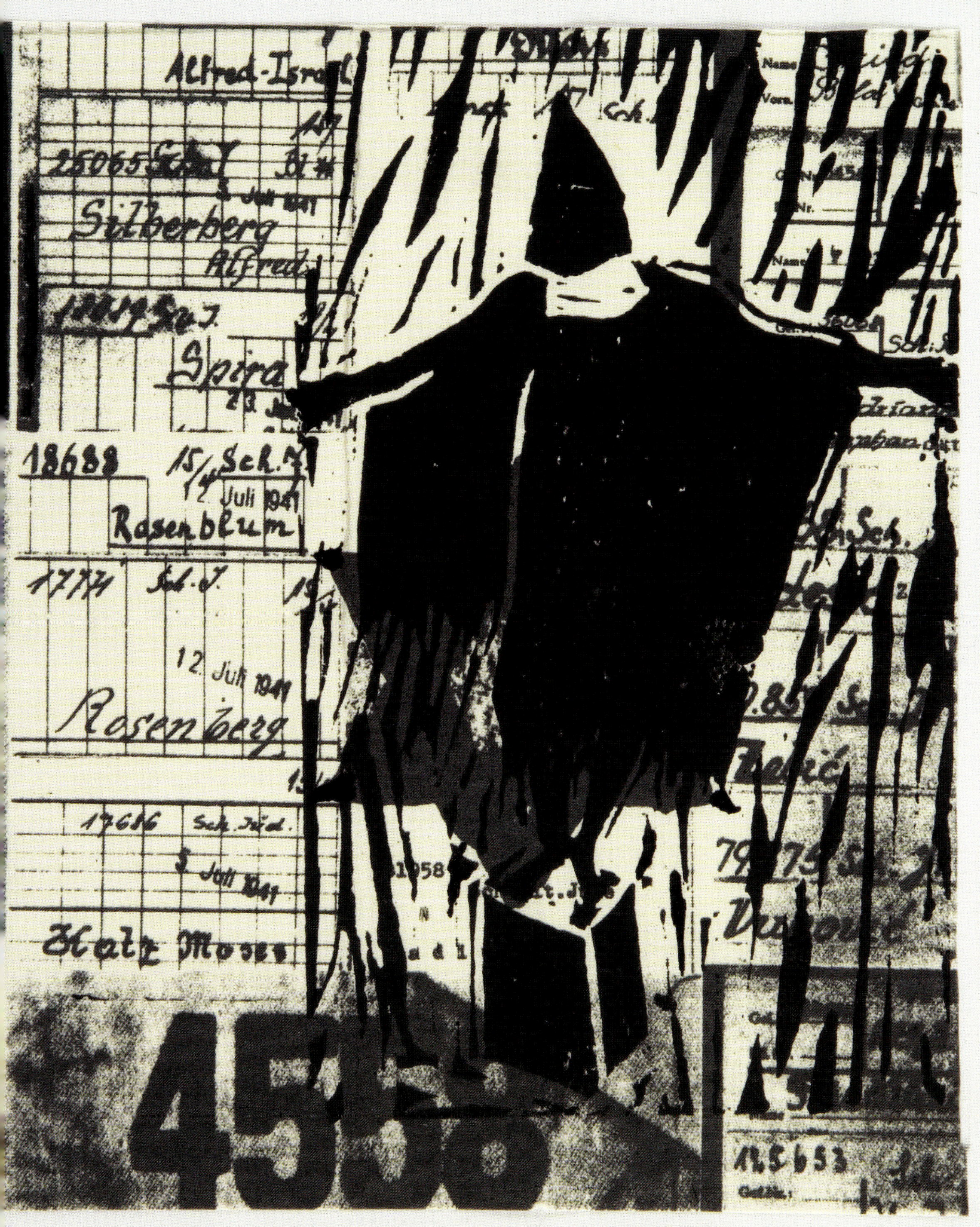
Alfred-Israel
Silberberg
Alfred
Spira
18688
Sch. J.
12. Juli 1941
Rosenblum
12. Juli 1941
Rosenberg
17686
Sch. Jüd.
5 Juli 1941
Katz Moses
125653

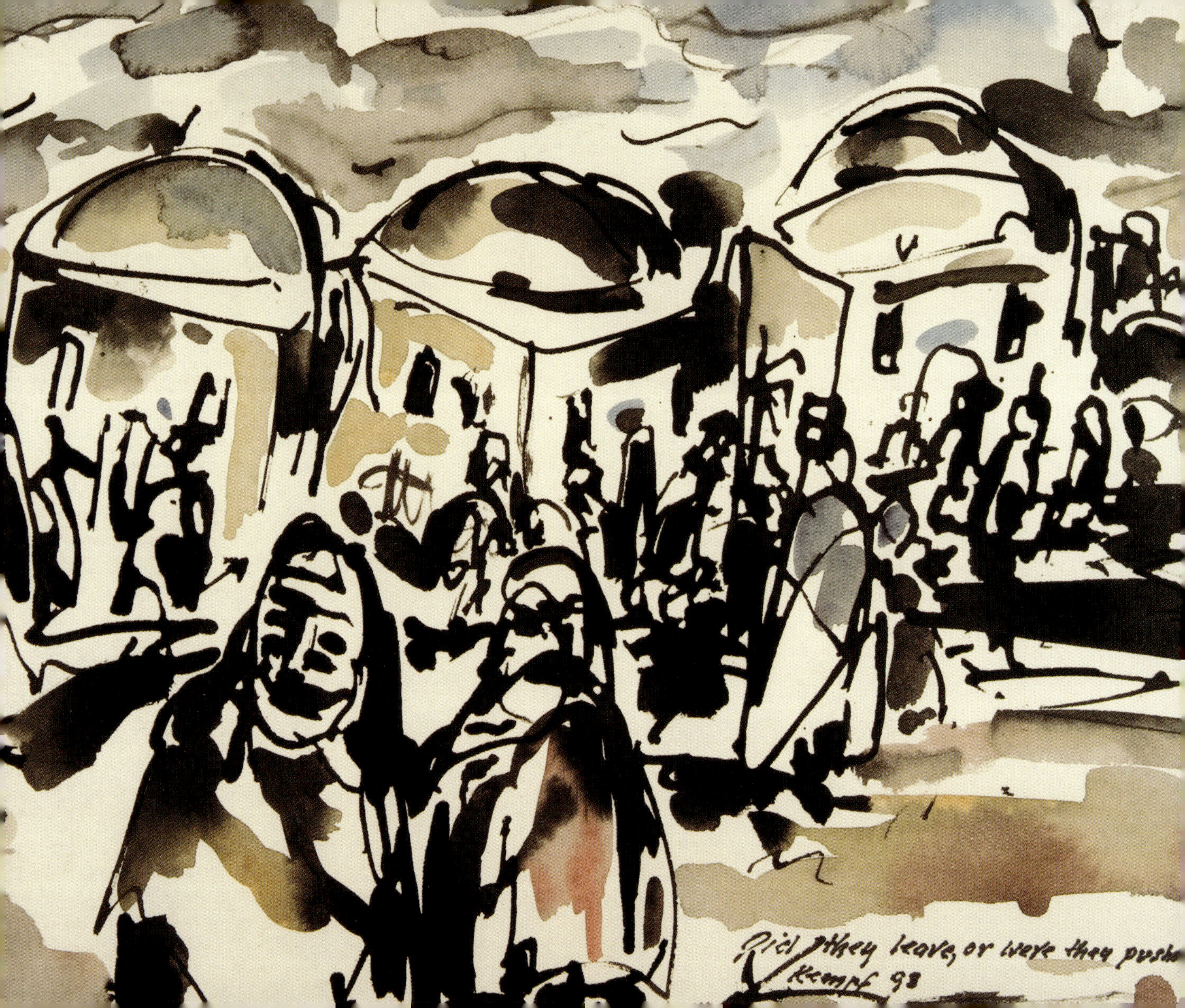
Did they leave, or were they pushe
Kempf 98

West Bank or *Did they leave or were they pushed?*

Do Palestinians feel less pain at the loss of a home, child or limb than those in Israel or Darfur?

December 2006: Unless we understand and have sympathy for those amongst us suffering privation and humiliation, what hope have we to concern ourselves with the grief and oppression of the many whom we only learn about by way of the media? It seems a lack of imagination that can allow these terrible crimes to take place without there being violent public protest. Indifference or double standards?

November 2006: Today our neighbours may be different in race, culture, colour or religion. Rather than this being a reason or excuse to perpetuate stereotypes, it is an opportunity for us to create a greater understanding of others, friendship and mutual respect.

It has been said that the Jewish evaluation of Christianity is a Jewish problem that can only be solved by dialogue and informed knowledge. That, I would suggest, also applies to our understanding of Islamic culture and religion.

February 2007: The State of Israel is not a state by divine right. As with any other state it is, or should be, subject to criticism for its political failures and the treatment of its citizens and neighbours, whatever their religion. Unfortunately, the raw or exposed nerves of many Zionists have a knee jerk reaction, falling back on the mindless response that any criticism of the state, no matter how well informed, is that the critic is either an anti-semite, or a self-hating Jew.

February 2007: I have a strong suspicion that the West and Israel believe they can reshape the Arab world. Before the Middle East is torn apart, survival remains with those prepared to negotiate, not liquidate. Understanding Spinoza would suggest: 'We affirm and deny many things because the nature of words allows us to affirm and deny, but not the nature of things, and therefore when this is not known we can easily take the false for the true.'

January 2009: Surely it is as possible to be a committed Jew whilst being critical of the Jewish state just as it is to be a loyal Australian and critical of government policy without being labelled un-Australian.

I recall my father saying: 'The party that is in opposition will always promise you the most.' That not only seems laconically Australian, but has elements of democratic realism.

2009: Nationalism, as (Heinrich) Heine (noted German poet and satirist of Jewish origin, who lived in the first half of the 19th century) has written, is the last resort of renegades and fools. We daily witness the monstrous crimes committed in the name of nationalism, fundamentalism, essentially ethnic cleansing.

6 November 2002: In Australia, if long overdue, we are concerned with the culture, the well-being and the advancement of the Aboriginal people. Equally, our moral concern should be with the Palestinians if there is ever to be peace in the land. A re-reading of the prophets Amos and Jeremiah may shed some light in the gathering gloom.

What hope, when the President of the Union of Orthodox Hebrew Congregations insists that Britain's Chief Rabbi, Jonathon Sacks, make atonement for his 'sin' and all copies of his book *The Dignity of Difference* be destroyed. Sacks rightly suggests that Israel is set on a tragic path.

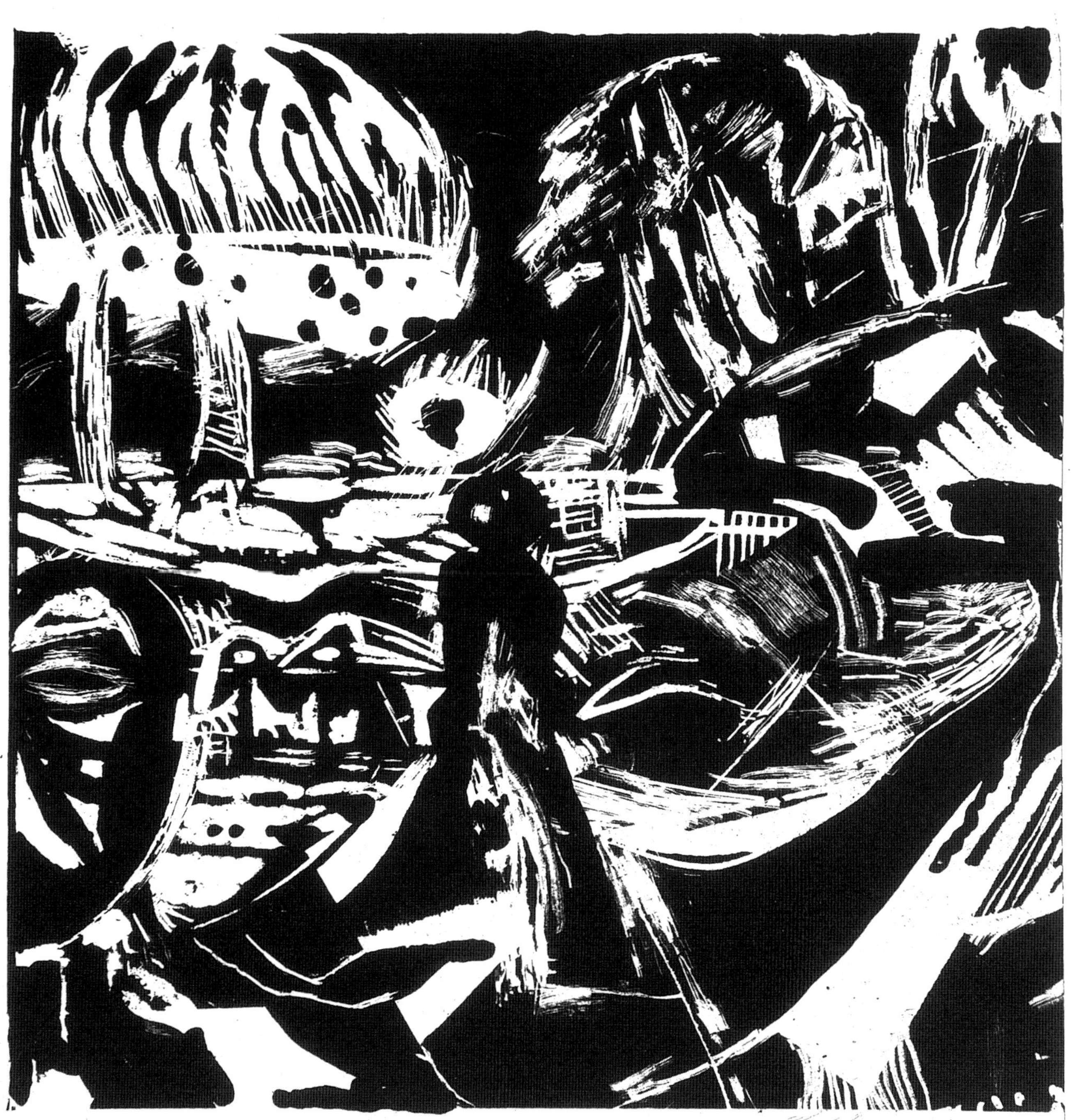
The Witness

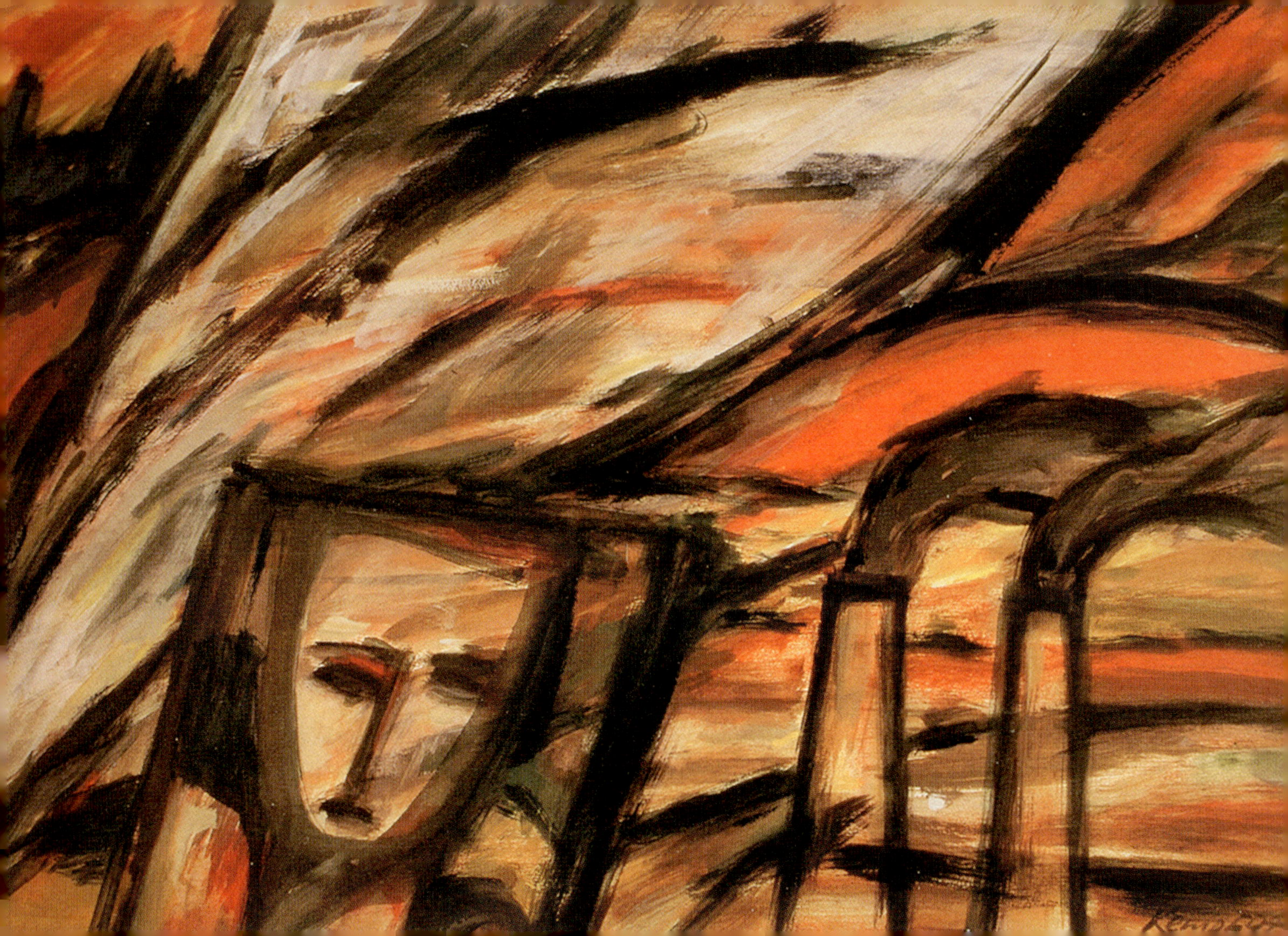

Memorial

I live in a world that is both entrancing and disturbing. Feeling a modicum of social responsibility, I attempt to covey information about the human condition. At times, this may be tranquil, expressive of an inner harmony, and often it will be expressive of a disquiet, reflecting disillusion with the human condition and its abject state. The demands made by these voices is constant throughout my work.

Forgotten

In the serenity of my studio whilst the temperature outside climbed and, unfortunately, continues to do so, it mirrors the political climate in the Middle East. As we took coffee, a massacre was taking place in a Jewish seminary.

Afterwards, seminarians outside were chanting: 'Death to the Arabs', whilst Palestinians celebrated the death of the students. Anti-Zionists continue to be both vocal and effective, stating: 'Zionists are not Jews'. It appears to me that states based on ethnicity ignore the fact that a minority of its citizens will be disadvantaged by being of a different race, or religion.

Considering the herd mentality of those supporting religion or political parties, what hope, even worse, religious parties!

Now we are to have another independent state in the Balkans, to quote Frank Campbell in the Australian: 'No matter that its gross domestic product is less than the takings of a milk bar and the national airline is a rented Cessna'.

It would be comic were it not so tragic.

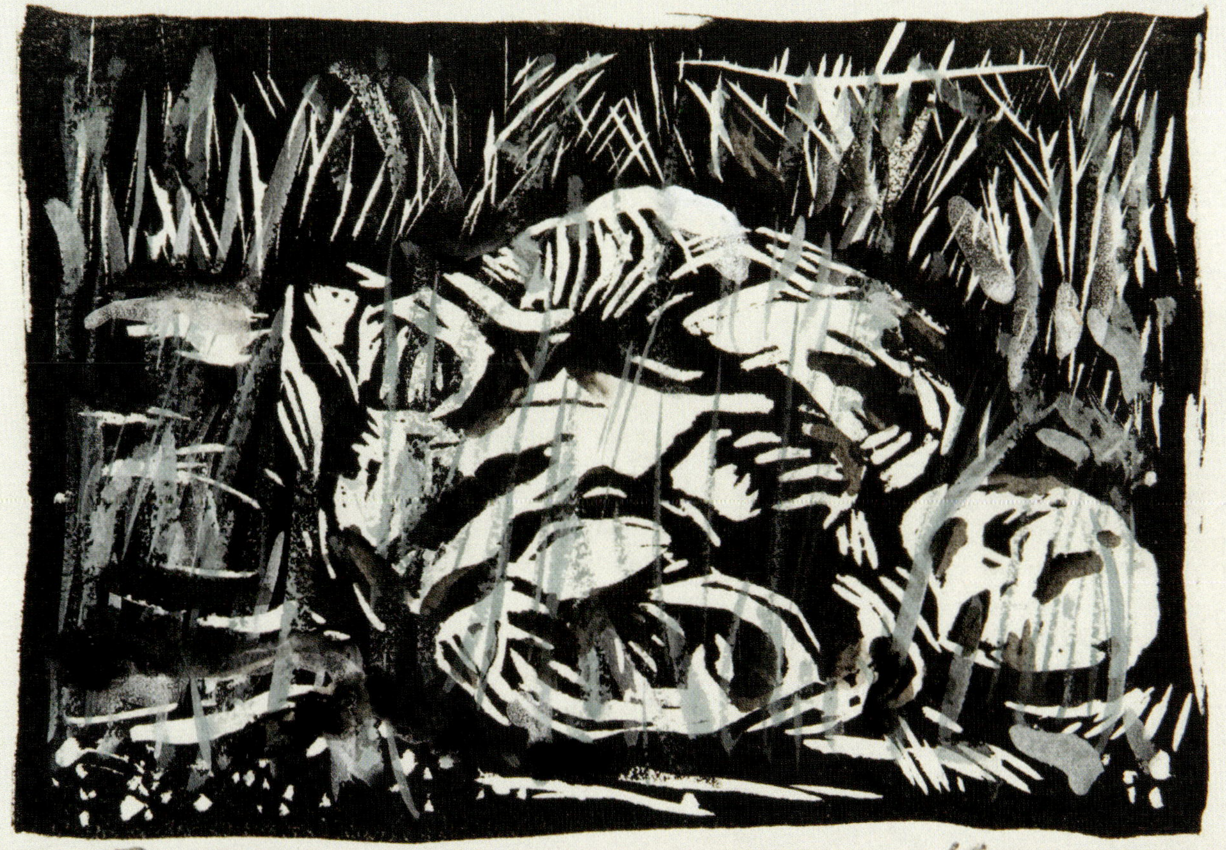

Forgotten   Kempf

The Last of the Just

Supposedly there are thirty-six just men – the *'Lamed Waf'* – who carry the sins of the world on their shoulders. In view of the tissue of lies and none-too-subtle fabrications we are expected to accept at face value, dodgy press releases designed to obfuscate the truth from weapons of mass destruction, Tampa and the children overboard, and more recently the Dr Haneef case.

It would appear that politicians and Federal Police are as kosher as their counterparts in Britain and the USA.

Daily we witness an erosion of human rights and civil liberties, a subtle and discernable corruption of free expression. It was appear that those thirty-six "just men" may be severely understaffed.

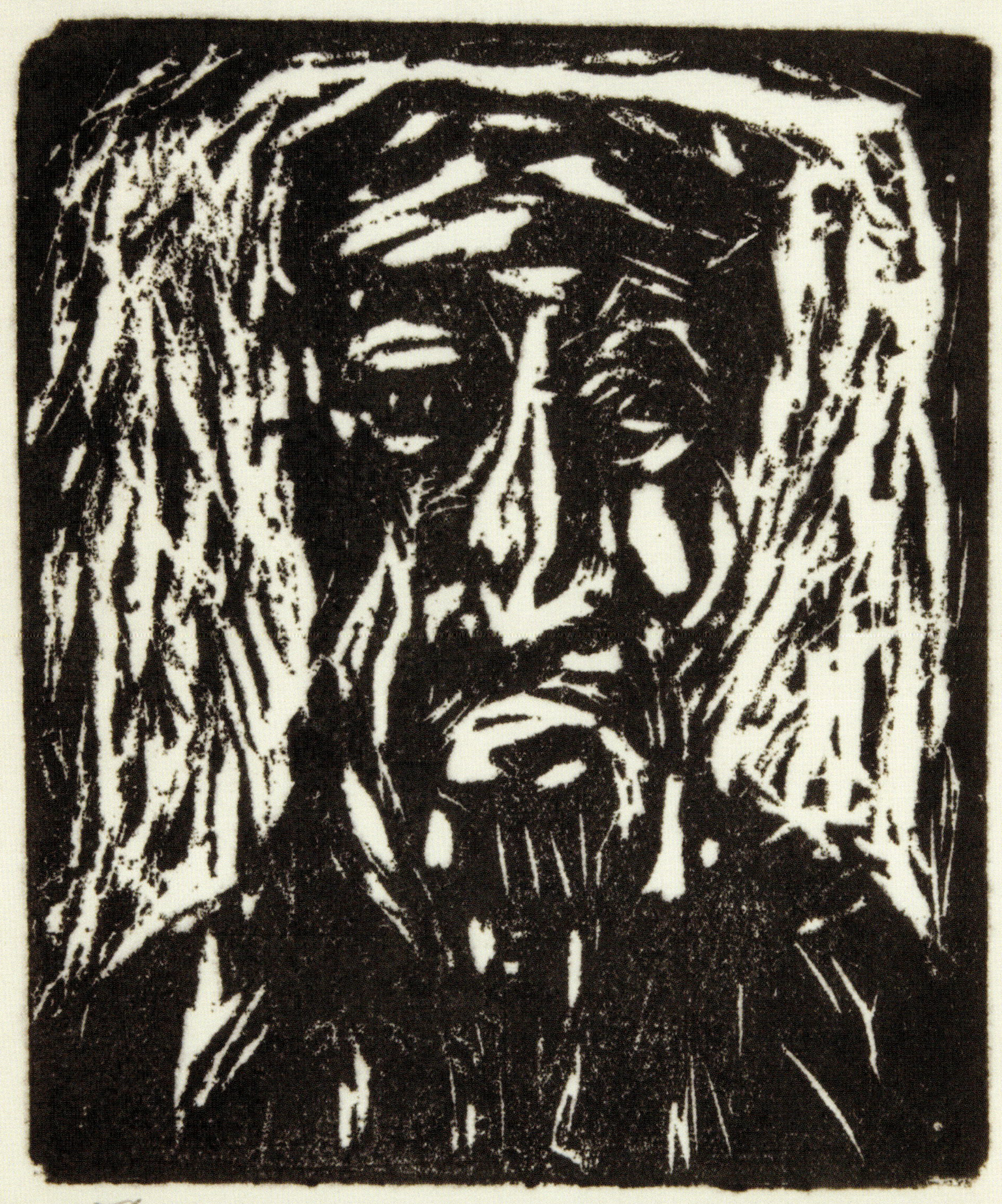

The Last of the Just Kempf

Jerusalem Tapestry

Jerusalem exerts a hold on the imagination like no other place. As I watch the sky darken over the old city from my studio at Miskenot Sha-ananamin, the cypress appear to reach to the heavens, connecting earth and sky. One feels that miracles did happen here. Maybe they still can. I commence my study for a 'Jerusalem Tapestry' …

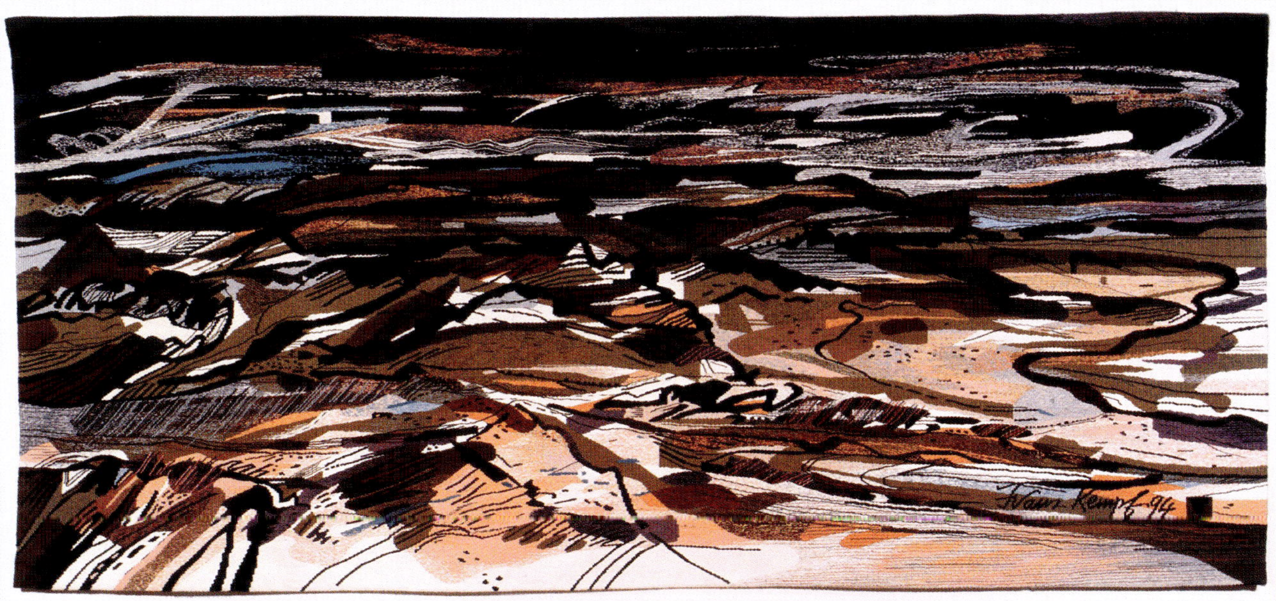

Always keep Ithaca fixed in your mind
To arrive there is your ultimate goal
But do not hurry the voyage at all
It is better to let it last for long years;
And even to anchor at the isle when you are old
Rich with all you have gained on the way
Not expecting that Ithaca will offer you riches
– CP Cavafy

Dead Man Walking/Unknown Soldier

2007: As I watched on television, Israelis coming to a standstill in the streets of Tel Aviv in respect to their fallen, I was reminded of my childhood, when the streets of Melbourne fell silent at the eleventh hour on Armistice Day; as we remembered the fallen in the War To End All Wars. What has changed? We continue to go on killing, or sending others to be killed. Politicians continue to exploit photo opportunity, expressing almost credible solidarity with those about to embark;

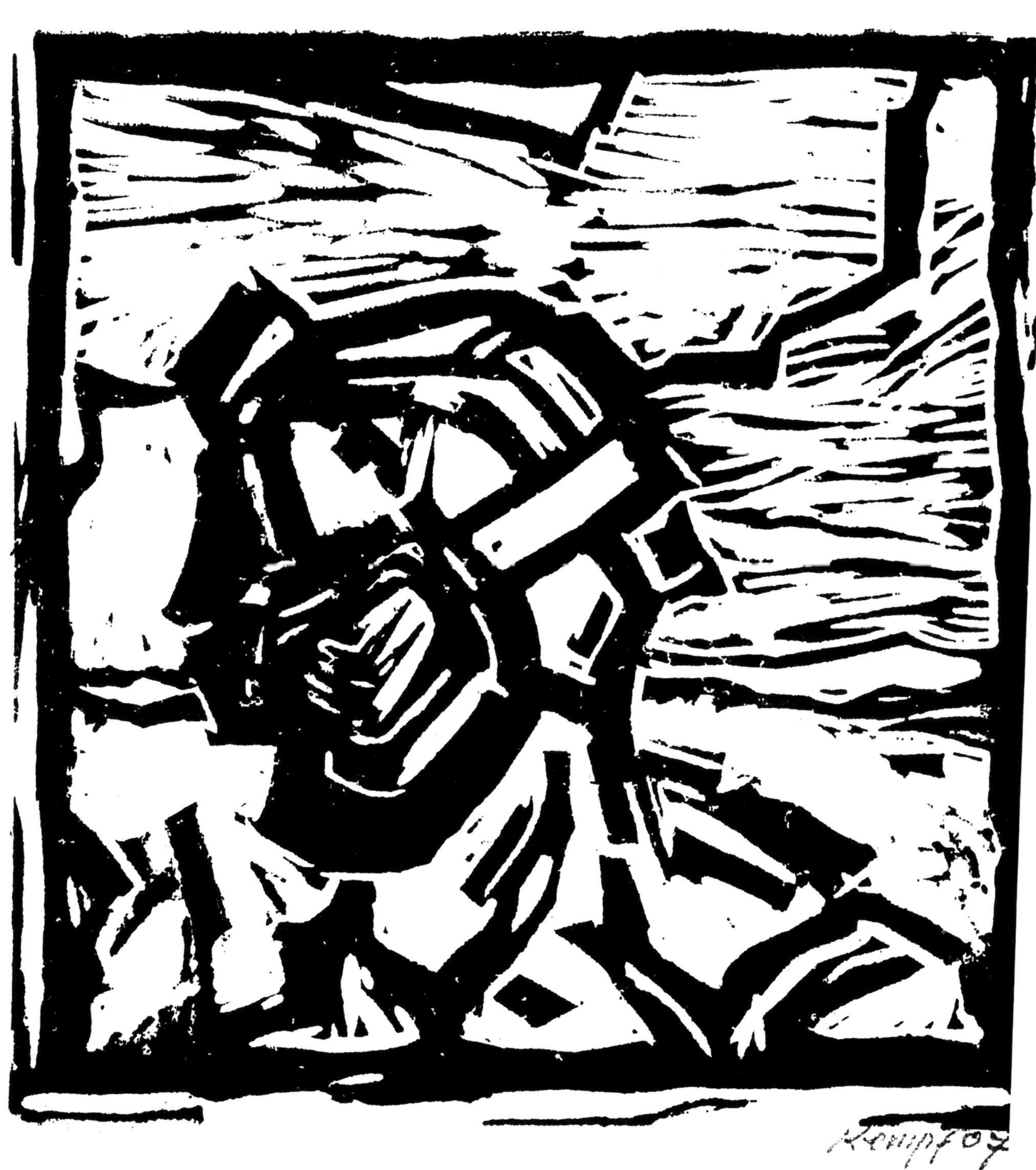
Kempf 07

to return home, traumatised from the carnage. It is reported that two thirds of U.S. servicemen return with neurological disorders, walking dead. Where are the Ministers of Defence and the media then? There is not much military chic when one's brains are rattling around in the skull. Do we then fall silent in the streets, remove our hats and bow our heads? Someone should!

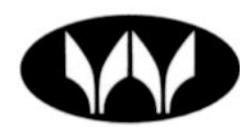

Wakefield Press is an independent publishing company based in Adelaide, South Australia. We love good stories and publish beautiful books. To see our full range of titles, please visit our website at www.wakefieldpress.com.au.